NR

D1446834

IN MY GOOD BOOKS

IN MY GOOD
BOOKS

by

V. S. PRITCHETT

KENNIKAT PRESS
Port Washington, N. Y./London

PN
710
.P7
1970

IN MY GOOD BOOKS

First published in 1942
Reissued in 1970 by Kennikat Press
Library of Congress Catalog Card No: 79-105823
ISBN 0-8046-0971-3

Manufactured by Taylor Publishing Company   Dallas, Texas

To

MY WIFE

Contents

CONTENTS

PREFACE

IF truth is the first casualty in war, the second is the literature of the period, especially the reflective literature. Why this should be so is plain enough. A war anticipates the gradual work of fashion and brings its medical date-stamp heavily down upon every contemporary book. It may be that the stamp will not last and that some books of the last twenty years will recover; but for the moment, they are "pre-war" or "between the wars"—as the saying is—and there is nothing for it but to watch them being trundled off to the sick-bay.

Two kinds of literature take their place: the topical and the classics. Of these the topical is the unhappier. Nothing dates so quickly as the latest news, and its lack of perspective becomes very soon intolerable. We turn to literature not only for respite, relaxation or escape from the boredom of reality and the gnaw of suffering, but to get away from uncertainty. And certainty is in the past. There, so it seems to us, things have been settled. There we can see a whole picture. For to see *something* whole becomes a necessity to people like ourselves whose world has fallen to pieces. Perhaps, we think, the certainty of the past will help our minds to substantiate a faith in the kind of certainty we hope for in the future.

That is one reason for reading the great literature of the past. I say "the great literature" not because of its aura of cultural strenuousness, but simply because, in the past, there is only great literature. Only the great stands the racket of time and survives from generation to generation; the rest dies for lack of staying power. But there is a second and painful reason why we should prepare ourselves for reading the great and intimidating masters: very soon there may be nothing else to read. Our contemporaries have almost ceased to write and, even if they begin again, it becomes every week more doubtful whether paper will be found to print them. The works of printers are bombed, books by the thousand are burned in the shops, stocks of paper are destroyed by fire or go to the bottom of the sea. Such incidents—to use the current euphemism for catastrophe—empty the purses of publishers, who may be forgiven for noting that living authors are expensive and that the dead, on the contrary, are cheap. The wise reader is one who prepares himself for the awful moment, a kind of Judgment Day, when only he and the hundred best authors are left in the world and have somehow to shake down together; when he will, so to speak, be stranded in the highest society. The conditions of modern journalism obliged us for years to proclaim one book in three a "masterpiece" or "a work of genius" and then, by the time the Blitz began in the autumn of 1940, we discovered our livelihood had gone. There were no more "masterpieces", there were not even any more books. We found ourselves left with the real masters. The essays in this book, most of which appeared in the *New Statesman and Nation* in slightly different form and length, describe the reactions of one critic, bookish but uneducated, to this unnerving situation.

I have said that one of the attractions which the great works of the past have for us is that they offer us the certainty of a completed world, a world finished and gone by. This is, of course, also one of the reasons why the classics repel us. The sentiment was well put by Huckleberry Finn, the patron saint of all lowbrows, who was not interested in the tale of "Moses and the Bulrushers" because "I don't take no stock of dead people". He "reckoned" he'd better "light out of the Territory" before Aunt Sally tried to "sivilise" him. "I can't stand it. I been there before." Even when we can stand a little more civilisation than Huck Finn cared for, we are likely to ask why on earth, in the twentieth century, we should read *Gil Blas*, *The Ring and the Book* or a novel by Benjamin Constant? The answer is that when we make our way through the sometimes old-fashioned curtain of words into the matter of the classics, we find that their serenity and certainty are misleading. The past is not serene. It is turbulent, upside down and unfinished. When we look into the lives of the authors of the great wise (or unwise) books, when we glance at the erratic outline of their times, we find that those men and those times were as uncertain as we are, and the picture they saw was by no means complete to their eyes. They lived— our hackneyed phrase is repeated throughout the history of literature—in "a period of transition". Every one of them had one foot in the old, the other in the new. If we pick up *Gulliver's Travels* again and, making an effort of imagination, pause to regard it as the new book it once was, we can feel it come to life in our hands, raw, unfinished, questioning and restless with its own disturbance. *There* is Swift at the beginning of modern science, *here* are we nearly two hundred years later, caught in all the consequences, some of which Swift foresaw. And the *Gulliver's Travels* we read will not be the childish abridgment of Lilliput nor the savage tale of the Houyhnhnms only; this time the episode on the island of Laputa, for years considered boring, and generally skipped, will stand out with fresh excitement and meaning.

What is true of Swift is true of most other classics, when we have rid ourselves of the notion that books are immaculately conceived or inspired and come down from heaven into the heads of writers. Nothing has really damned the classics so thoroughly in the mind of the ordinary reader as the idea that they are "inspired". A work of art is an act of co-operation, often of reluctant co-operation like an awkward marriage, between an author and the kind of society he lives in. When we know something of the character of this aggravating partner, that which was once stiff and monumental becomes fluid and alive.

The most satisfying classics at present are those in which the cries of an age are like echoes of our own. In all the literature of the French Revolution, through the Napoleonic wars to the Reform, we find books which seem to be describing our own times. At no other period has Napoleonic literature from the novel of Benjamin Constant to the works of writers as diverse as Erckmann-Chatrian or Cobbett, had the freshness, the significance and pleasure we find in it now. Everything is there from Bloomsbury of the twenties to the recriminations of the thirties and the fighting of this war. We hold up the crystal sphere; we see ourselves in miniature reflection and, perhaps, if our minds are not too literal, we may also see our future. The time of the Civil War offers vaguer but still apposite comparisons. We look back from Hemingway to Defoe, from modern non-attachment to the dynamic quietism of George Fox. In the middle of the eighteenth century, Fielding draws a Fuehrer. I do not suggest that such comparisons will always be found in these essays; but in the numerous cases of wide difference, in Le Sage, Synge or Zola, to take random examples, the differences take on meaning when we turn from literary criticism to a consideration of the social background of the authors. Our pleasure in literature is increased by knowing that a book is the fruit of living in a certain way. The mind of Browning is boring until we consider it as one of the manifestations of the violent Victorian unrest, and a period piece like *The Diary of a Nobody* ceases to die of its own triviality when it is related to its period.

I am an unsystematic reader and the subjects of these essays have been chosen at random. They make no case. The accident of finding an author handy on the shelf has usually decided me. I owe an especial debt to Mr. Raymond Mortimer for his many suggestions. At the end of the book the reader will find a note on where he can pick up the works discussed.

GIBBON AND THE HOME GUARD

"No war has had greater results on the history of the world or brought greater triumphs to England," writes the historian Green when he comes to the Seven Years War, "but few have had more disastrous beginnings." To that familiar note we are now inured. Military preparedness appears to be an impossibility in these islands. At the beginning of 1756 there were only three regiments fit for service, and after the collapse of the Duke of Cumberland's army on the Elbe a year later "a despondency without parallel in our history took possession of our coolest statesmen, and even the impassive Chesterfield cried in despair, 'We are no longer a nation'." So often has the despondency been paralleled since, and so often survived, that one hesitates to repeat the old, old story for fear of encouraging the gloomy smugness of it once too often. There were 18,000 men waiting to cross the Channel at Quiberon in the summer of 1759, before Admiral Hawke scotched them. But now, in contrast to the despair of two years earlier, "the national spirit most gloriously disproved the charge of effeminacy which, in a popular estimate, had been imputed to the times".

Edward Gibbon wrote these words when he looked back upon the military ardour which penetrated to the sleepy hesitations of country life at Buriton, near Petersfield, and which impelled his father to drive both of them into the Militia:

> The country rings around with loud alarms,
> And raw in fields the rude Militia swarms.

Gibbon remembered his Dryden. Left to himself, removed

from his notorious habit of "obeying as a son", Gibbon (one suspects) would have stayed where he was with his nose in his books and raising an occasional eye to consider and dismiss the prospect of marrying the next imperfect West Sussex lady on the calling list. Perhaps if he had not joined the Home Guard of 1759 Gibbon might have married from lack of having anything else to do, and then—who knows—we might be reading of the Birth and Rise, rather than of the Decline and Fall of the Roman Empire. A woman, even one of the West Sussex chatterboxes, might have prevailed against the eighteenth-century taste for ruins. But Gibbon *père* had always been the decisive partner in the life of Gibbon *fils*. The father had put his foot down once or twice to some effect already; and having sent the youth to the Continent in order to rid him of Popery, he was equally determined on effacing the Frenchified personality and mind which the young man had brought back in exchange for his religion. Edward Gibbon was to be made into an Englishman, and on June 12th Major and Captain Gibbon received their commissions in the South Battalion of the Hampshires.

The story of Gibbon's service with the Militia is well known. It can be read in his *Autobiography*, in his *Journal*, and in the various *Lives*, of which Mr. D. M. Low's is especially thorough, sympathetic and readable. To the one-time Territorial, the conscript or the Home Guard of today Gibbon's experiences are amusing, consoling and instructive. The peculiar torments which sting the amateur soldier seem to change very little from age to age. Joining to repel the invader at a moment's notice, the Gibbons were very soon to find that the Navy had done it for them—Hawke sank the French at Quiberon in the following November—and that their patriotism had led them into the demoralising trap of soldiering without an enemy. Gibbon's first impression confirmed the remaining lines of Dryden:

14

Mouths without hands maintained at vast expense,
In peace a charge, in war a weak defence.
Stout once a month they march, a blust'ring band,
And ever but in times of need at hand.
This was the more when, issuing on guard,
Drawn up in rank and file they stood prepar'd,
Of seeming arms to make a short essay;
Then hasten to be drunk—the business of the day.

As a writer, Gibbon found himself in charge of the battalion's administrative and even literary affairs, which meant mainly conducting the correspondence and piling up the dossier of a row—"passionate and prolix"—a typical military row with a peer about precedence. When the danger of invasion had passed, the Major and the Captain hoped to be allowed to take their duties easily in Petersfield or Alton, but they were caught for two and a half years more and began an unheroic, tedious and often sordid progress round the South of England. Winchester was too near home for discipline; they went to Devon, where they were happy, to Devizes where the habits of the town were riotous—twenty-one courts-martial—to Porchester, where they guarded the French prisoners and many of the men caught fevers or the smallpox in the swampy wildernesses nearby, to Alton, where they entered the camp "indisputably the last and worst".

To the Major this was all far less depressing than to the Captain. There was a vein of happy impetuosity and slackness in the Major's character. He had always been at home in either the highest or the lowest society. He frequently cut parades, and when he did turn up his drill was terrible. Gibbon writes: "We had a most wretched field day. Major, officers and men seemed to try which should do worst." The Captain did not claim to be perfect: "The battalion was out, officers but no powder. It was the worst field day we had had a good

while, the men were very unsteady, the officers very inatten-
tive, and I myself made several mistakes." Still, there were
consolations: "After going through the manual, which they
did with great spirit, I put them . . . thro' a variety of evolutions. . . . At the volley I made them recover their arms,
not a piece went off." Edward Gibbon was not one of those
lackadaisical literary soldiers who hope their shufflings and
errors will be lost in the crowd or that their sporadic brainwaves will impress the command. He was, as always, thorough,
industrious and responsible; and some part of his suffering was
due to his conscientiousness.

The qualities we expect of Gibbon are sense, balance and
judiciousness. No man is more likely to give a more considered account of his experience, to extract the value from
his disappointments, to gather in, perhaps complacently, all the
compensations. The plump little man, only five feet high,
with the bulging forehead and the bulbous cheeks, gazes like
some imperturbable and learned baby at his life and can be
trusted to give both sides of the question, if only for the sensuous
pleasure of balancing a sentence:

> The loss of so many busy and idle hours was not compen-
> sated by any elegant pleasure; and my temper was insensibly
> soured by the society of our rustic officers who were alike
> deficient in the knowledge of scholars and the manners of
> gentlemen. In every state there exists, however, a balance
> of good and evil. The habits of a sedentary life were usefully
> broken by the duties of an active profession; in the healthful
> exercise of the field I hunted with a battalion instead of
> a pack, and at that time I was ready at any hour of the day
> or night to fly from quarters to London, from London to
> quarters on the slightest call of private or regimental business.
> But my principal obligation to the militia was the making
> me an Englishman and a soldier. After my foreign educa-
> tion, with my reserved temper, I should long have continued
> a stranger in my native country, had I not shaken in this

various scene of new faces and new friends; had not experience forced me to feel the characters of our leading men, the state of parties, the forms of office, and the operation of our civil and military system. In this peaceful service I imbibed the rudiments of the language and science of tactics which opened a new field of study and observation. . . . The discipline and evolutions of a modern battalion gave me a clearer notion of the Phalanx and the Legions, and the Captain of the Hampshire Grenadiers [the reader may smile] has not been useless to the historian of the Roman Empire.

He took Horace with him on the march and read up the questions of Pagan and Christian theology in his tent. Sooner or later, the great men turn out to be all alike. They never stop working. They never lose a minute. It is very depressing.

Gibbon, like Francis Bacon, Swift and Dr. Johnson, is a writer whose experience is digested and set forth like the summing-up of a moral judge. "My temper is not very susceptible of enthusiasm" . . . that is not really quite true, as his sudden conversion to Rome, his first meetings with Suzanne Curchod, his occasional feats with the bottle at Lausanne and in the militia seem to show. But if not phlegmatic, he is formal. The truth is that his temper was far more susceptible to style. For him style was the small, ugly man's form of power. His shocking health as a child and youth, though astonishingly restored when he was sixteen years of age, must have inscribed on his heart and instincts the detachment, the reserve, the innate melancholy of invalid habits. The coldness which is alleged, the tepidity of feeling and the fixed air of priggishness and conceit, are misleading. Really, he is self-contained. In telling his own story he is not recklessly candid, but he is honest to a startling extent, and especially in disclaiming emotions which it is conventional to claim. His formality is comic, even intentionally so at times, and his detachment about himself may, of course, show an

17

unconscionable vanity; but it also indicates the belief that a civilised man is one who ought to be able to stand the display of all the evidence. We think here particularly of his brief comment on Rousseau's dislike of his character and behaviour: Rousseau, Gibbon mildly remarks, ought not to have passed judgment on a foreigner. (Or did Gibbon mean that a continental enthusiast ought not to pass judgment on an English country gentleman? It is quite likely he did mean this.) Gibbon is not ashamed to record his constant concern about money and property, nor to admit that his father's recklessness about money alarmed him not only as a son, but as an heir. And after drawing the most gracious portrait of his father, he is careful not to end on the note of filial idolatry or remorse:

> The tears of a son are seldom lasting. I submitted to the order of Nature, and my grief was soothed by the conscious satisfaction that I had discharged all the duties of filial piety. Few perhaps are the children who, after the expiration of some months or years, would sincerely rejoice in the resurrection of their parents; and it is a melancholy truth, that my father's death, not unhappy for himself, was the only event that could save me from an hopeless life of obscurity and indigence.

It *is* a melancholy truth. Gibbon has a taste for the truth that is melancholy, for seeing life as a series of epitaphs. And yet in Reynolds' portrait the fat little scholar with the second roll of chin, and the lips which seem set for the discharge of some destructive epigram, is not as sober as he looks. He is, in fact, cutting a dash. With the amateur soldier's love of a splash and with a glance back at the heroic days when his Militia boldly exercised within sight of the French coast, he has put on his scarlet coat for the picture. "For in England the red ever appears the favourite and, as it were, the national colour of our military ensigns and uniforms."

A CONSCRIPT

CONSCRIPTION for military service, in peace and war, has not a long history in Europe. It dates from the French Revolution and was the basis of Napoleon's enormous military achievement. No other general in Europe could say, as he did to Metternich: "I can afford to lose 30,000 men per month." But many years passed before a population who had been used to the unheroic pleasures of peaceful industry and were far removed from memory of the massacres of the religious wars, became amenable to this pace of slaughter. Men fled from their houses in thousands, the Vendée rose in revolt. Nevertheless in times of revolutionary persecution and espionage, the army becomes the safest hiding-place; the glory of the Napoleonic conquests was irresistible and, with all Europe hungry, the discovery that you could pillage the conquered and live well off them, was a final factor in making for the success of the new system. One has only to look at the memoirs of such rogues as Vidocq to see what a piping time the tougher conscripts had. Their European travels turned them into foreigners. They became a race apart. This is of course true of all soldiers. In his *Verdun* M. Jules Romains shows that the common daydream of the men in the trenches was of somehow melting away from the front in little bands, retiring to the woods and living a kind of Robin Hood life on the tribute they exacted from civilians.

What was the life of Napoleon's first European conscripts? Some idea can be got from that old school-book, *Histoires d'un Conscrit de 1813*, by Erckmann-Chatrian. (It is a pity one reads these two Alsatian authors at school, for while they are safe enough and exciting enough for schoolboys and inculcate a very sound and civilised moral repugnance to Cæsarism, they have a quality which schoolboys are not able to appreciate.) Neither Chatrian, the glassmaker who worked his way up in the world, and became a school teacher, nor Erckmann, the clever briefless lawyer, were actually Napoleonic conscripts. They were born a few years after Waterloo and they wrote of the campaigns and the revolution itself as those events still lived in the memories of their elders, picking up the old boasts and lamentations from humble and ordinary folk. They look at the war from below, assume in their stories the point of view of some small tradesman or peasant, and view the scene from the vantage-point of a period of disillusion. This pretence of being eye-witnesses and with it the circumstantial manner at which they excel, recalls Defoe's *Journal of the Plague Year*. Both books have that modest, trim, but firm respectability, the stoicism of the small trader. The meek shall inherit the earth. Joseph, the good, lame apprentice working overtime to save up money in order to marry his innocent little Catherine whose hand he holds all the evening like a sugar stick, is an early example of the pious, non-tough hero of the nineteenth century. He does not seem a prig to us because he is good without knowing it, or perhaps one should say that really his piety lies not in his religion but in an innate belief in the goodness of his class itself. (In popular belief class is the chief God.) Sainte Beuve scornfully called this book "L'Iliade de la peur", but if Joseph is often as frightened as any young soldier is, he is certainly no coward. He stands his ground in the French squares, terrified by the screaming, monkey faces of the Prussian Hussars as they charge down at the Battle of Leipzig, but he is savagely angry that any man on earth should try and take away his life without consulting him and in a cause to which he is indifferent. "La gloire" did not intoxicate Joseph. Before he went to his medical examinations he swallowed a bottleful of vinegar, hoping to deceive the doctors, because he had been told this drink would make him look as pale as an invalid. In fact it gave him the violent flush of an enormous health, and he regards his failure to get out of military service as a just punishment for acting a lie. Mild, one would call Joseph, very mild, yet really he has the pathos which war gives to the sensible man:

> I wish those who love glory so much would go and find it themselves and not leave it to others.
>
> To tell you the truth [said Zebedee] I think the same as you do, but as they have got us it is better to say we are fighting for glory.

One reads all books on the Napoleonic period with one eye continually jumping forward to the present. The pacifist would naturally jump at a passage like the one I have quoted; but the moral of the book is not pacific. It is patriotic denunciation of despotism, and it is based upon descriptions of what the ordinary man and woman were saying and feeling at the time. Here I think those who are conducting anecdotal propaganda in Germany against Hitler might read the *Story of a Conscript* with advantage. It is a book full of fruitful murmurs and suggestive ironies. Joseph joins up after the retreat from Moscow, and a wonderful public statement is issued in the town admitting and indeed almost boasting of the catastrophe and calling for more sacrifices.

I quote from R. G. Gillman's translation in the Everyman Edition:

> Harmentier, the police sergeant, came from the watch-house and stood on the top of the steps, with a large piece of paper in his hand, similar to that which was placed on the wall; some soldiers were with him. Everybody ran towards him, but the soldiers made them stand back. Harmentier began by reading the notice, which he called the

29th bulletin, in which the Emperor stated that, during the retreat from Moscow, the horses had died every night by thousands; he said nothing about the men. As the sergeant read slowly and more slowly, the listeners whispered never a word; even the old woman listened dumbly like the rest, although she could not understand French.

The silence was such that one could hear a pin drop. When the sergeant came to this passage: "Our cavalry were so utterly disorganised that it was necessary to form the officers who still had a horse left, into four companies of one hundred and fifty men each; the generals and colonels acting as regimental officers, and those of lower rank as privates". When he read this, which spoke more than anything for the sufferings of the Grande Armée, I heard groans and cries on every side, and two or three women fell to the ground and had to be helped away.

The notice terminated with these words: "The health of his Majesty has never been better." This was indeed one great consolation to us; unhappily, this consolation could not bring back to life the 300,000 men buried in the snow, and the people went away very, very sad.

Before the disaster in Russia became known the simple people of Alsace believed that, since Napoleon had conquered the whole of Europe, the war would be over. "You forget," the sardonic replied, "that there is still the conquest of China." One can imagine that being said in Germany. Erckmann-Chatrian were, it is true, writing tendenciously after the event; but after all, France had seen the revolution betrayed, and had paid a frightful price for her Fuehrer. At the summit of conquest there is always uncertainty and guilt in the minds of the conqueror's followers. "It can't last." "We shall have to pay." But Joseph found himself shouting "Vive l'Empereur" with the rest, and could not explain why he shouted with such fervour for the man who had enslaved him.

The conscripts of 1813 and the conscripts today have very

much the same experiences. Joseph and his friends soon found themselves standing drinks to the old soldiers, whose thirst was boundless. The veterans were patronising and the conscripts were cocky. Duels between them were common. The second lesson was the foundation of military discipline:

> The corporal is always right when he speaks to the private soldier, the sergeant is right when he speaks to the corporal, the sergeant-major is right when speaking to the sergeant, the sub-lieutenant to the sergeant-major, and so on upwards to the marshall of France—even if he were to say that the moon shines in broad daylight or that two and two make five.
>
> This is not an easy thing to get into your head, but there is one thing which is a great help to you, and that is a great noticeboard fixed up in the rooms, and which is read out from time to time, to settle your thoughts. This notice-board enumerates everything that a soldier is supposed to want to do—such as, for instance, to return to his native village, to refuse service, to contradict his superior officer, etc., and always ends by promising he shall be shot or at least have five years hard labour, with a cannon ball fastened to his leg if he does it.

You then sold your civilian clothing and stood the corporals more drinks "as it is well to be friends with them, as they drilled us morning and afternoon in the courtyard". And the drinks were served by one Christine, an eternal figure.

> She showed particular consideration for all young men of good family, as she called those who were not careful of their money. How many of us were fleeced to their last sou in order to be called "men of good family".

Joseph has no private adventures or affairs on the way. He is the normal prig, the prudent Mr. Everyman, who keeps as far from trouble as he can. He is thinking all the time of his dear Catherine; but Catherine, you feel pretty certain, is not going to be like the rest of the Phalsbourg girls, who turn round and marry someone else the moment their young man joins up and goes away. Joseph's day-long hope is that he won't be in the advance guard, that he won't have to kneel in the front rank of the square when the cavalry charge; and when he gets to billets he is worried about the state of his feet and always manages to awaken the sympathy of the household. The odd thing is that he has our sympathy too. Erckmann-Chatrian succeed in making us prefer Joseph to the rasher and more virile Zebedee who fights a duel with a veteran and kills him with his sabre. The reason for this preference is that Joseph, in his mildness, is exactly the right kind of narrator. His virtue after all is not that of the best boy in the Sunday School; it is the virtue of everyday life, the *virtu* of peace set against the *virtu* of war. Such a humble figure shows up the gaudy chaos of war in dramatic contrast. The excellence of Erckmann-Chatrian lies in their continual remembrance of the common human feelings; and in the midst of their battle pieces, as the grape-shot ploughs the ranks and the men take up positions in the upper rooms of cottages, or in the horrible scenes of surgery which occur afterwards, the authors are always exact about the feeling of the simple man. Who does not respond to Joseph's description of his first action when he came under artillery fire?—

A tremendous cloud of smoke surrounded us and I said to myself if we remain here a quarter of an hour longer we shall be killed without a chance of defending ourselves. It seemed hard that it should be so.

Another point that occurs to me when I read either this book or *L'Histoire d'un Paysan* (a book which describes all the phases of the revolution as they affected a peasant), is that the modern literature of war and revolution has become too egotistical. What "I" said, what "I" did, what happened to "me". The modern books from Blunden to Hemingway are all far more horrifying than Erckmann-Chatrian and I wonder how much this is due to their exceptional, personal point of view. For I do not think that the entire explanation is that modern war has become more horrifying. Erckmann-Chatrian can be grim. There is the moment, for example, when a soldier will not believe he has lost his arm until he sees it lying among a pile of amputated arms and recognises it by the tattoo mark. But usually the authors are sparing with this kind of particularity. Although a conscript or a peasant is writing, the predominant pronoun is "we" not "I"; he is writing of *all* the peasants, *all* his friends, *all* the soldiers. The private sensibility is merged with the general and we get a sensibility to the feelings of crowds, classes and masses which was to become one of the marks of nineteenth-century literature and which we have lost. When Erckmann-Chatrian were writing, this had not degenerated into the only too convenient means of melodrama and the vague picturesque. The simplicity and sincerity of the eighteenth century gave the Erckmann-Chatrian "we" a real humanity, a genuine sentiment, a moral charm. The tough, first-person-singular hero of today is rich in knowingness; he knows the ropes far better than a softie like Joseph; but the tough man is poor in feeling, for the Romantic movement has intervened to make his feelings seem both larger and more catastrophically injured than they really are. . . . Morbidity and insincerity are never far off. This poverty of feeling has affected the tough man's awareness of his comrades, for he is afraid of betraying himself before them. Our impression, in fact, is that the tough man is more afraid of his friends than of his enemies—a falsification of soldierly character which the "soft school" were incapable of making.

A SWISS NOVEL

THE difficulty, in thinking about *Adolphe*, is to lay the ghost of Constant. One is listening to Mozart against a disruptive mutter of music-hall which has got on to almost the same wavelength. But this happens with all the Romantics; their passionate exaltation of the first person singular aimed at the solitary *cri de cœur* but it leaves one with a confusing impression of duet, in which life, with its subversive pair of hands, is vamping in jaunty undertone the unofficial version. Beside the broken heart of the imagined Ellenore, healed at last by death, stands Madame de Staël, in the full real flesh of her obstreperous possessiveness with no sign of mortality on her. She is off to Germany to write a damned good book. And as Adolphe, free at last, contemplates with horror the wilderness of his liberty, up bobs Constant, explanatory about his secret marriage, still hopelessly susceptible, still with a dozen duels before him on account of ladies' faces and with one leg out of the nuptial couch at the thought of the rather acid entice-ments of Madame Recamier. It is distressing that a man should obtrude so persistently on his own confessions.

One of the earliest psychological novelists, Constant is enmeshed in ambiguity. He is more than the surgeon of the heart; he is more than the poet of masochism. *Adolphe* is not the tragedy of unequal love created out of the comedy of his chronic amorousness: it is the tragedy of the imagination itself and rendered in words as melodiously and mathematically clear as the phrases of a Mozart quartet. One understands as one reads *Adolphe* why the tears streamed down Constant's face and why his voice choked when he read the book. But he did weep rather a lot. He went weeping about the Courts of Europe with it—taking his precautions. Would Madame de Staël object to this line? Had he sufficiently toned down the money difficulties? (One would like to write the financial side of *Adolphe*, but that kind of thing was left to the vulgar Balzac.) Had he beaten up his literary omelette so well that none of his wives and mistresses could put out a finger and exclaim, Lo! here, or Lo! there? He was very anxious and very evasive. Never can autobiography—disguised though it was—have emerged from the facts with such a creeping and peeping. There was even a special preface for the English edition, in which, knowing his England, he declared *Adolphe* was a cautionary tale to warn us of the wretchedness of love which tries to live outside the necessary conventions of society. There is a sort of sincerity in this, of course; Constant had the bullied free-lover's sneaking regard for marriage as a kind of patent medicine. The dictatorship of Napoleon and the despotism of Madame de Staël had given him a hunger for the constitutional. But for one who thought nobly of the soul he is—well, shall we say, practical?

One looks up from the music of *Adolphe*, from the cool dissertation of that unfaltering violin, to the noble head of his portrait. At Holland House, when they watched him, aware that they were being entertained by one of the most intelligent scandals of exiled Europe, they must have noticed that he had none of the frank charlatanry of the Romantics. A dignified and even debonair forty, he was sensitive, witty and vivacious. The nose suggests firmness and probity. And yet one can understand that Constant was considered a shade tough. One detects the buried outline of the original human monkey under the half-smile of the small courtier. In the pose and in the eyes there is something of the mandrill's mask, something of that animal's vanity and temper. So gentle—and yet Ellenore and Madame de Staël, violent themselves, complain of the

27

rasp of his tongue. The mouth is almost beautiful, a talker's mouth caught with the perpetual epigram, but it lifts at the corner with an upward twist of slyness. It hints at the hard malice of the inhibited. One does not altogether trust Constant even before one has read *Adolphe*. One foresees the danger of a cleverness which is indecisive, the peril of an elusiveness which is captivating but never revealing.

What is lacking in the portrait is any sign of the morbid apathy of his nature. M. Gustav Rudler, the most searching editor of *Adolphe*, says Constant lived in a sort of apathy which "made crises of passion an essential need". A cat-and-dog life with all those mistresses, duels with young Englishmen—he was still at it in his crippled old age, being carried to the ground to fire from his chair—a wicked senility at the gaming tables. "I leave myself to Chance," Constant wrote, "I go where it puts me and stay there until it sweeps me away again." Brilliant and unrevealing in conversation, he buries his serious opinions which he can contemplate only when he is alone. And then the temperature is so cool that the sensibility is still thwarted and unmelted. He lives listlessly and constrained. This is Byronism once more, the beginning of the malady of the age; but Byronism turned analytical, without the guts, without also the hocus-pocus. His world weariness has no sense of theatre; it is not so highly coloured; it is the fatigue which makes for the abstract mind and not for poetic journalism, the sickness of the *âmes sèches*.

"Je ne puis que vous plaindre", the father of Adolphe writes when he observes that, as he expected, the young man's determination to break with Ellenore is going to weaken. "Je ne puis que vous plaindre de ce qu'avec votre esprit d'indépendance, vous faites toujours ce que vous ne voulez pas." But lovers of independence are like that; the love of liberty is more easily come by than the will to ensue it. Constant was inured to despotism; society conspired with Madame de Staël to reduce his will. Adolphe and Constant together both lament their lack of career. And if one can think of the writer of a masterpiece as a failure, the *âme sèche* of Constant was not the sole or even the chief cause of his disorientation. It is true that Madame de Staël's party was the wrong one to belong to; but it was anyway hopeless for Constant to be a liberal democrat, full of the ideas of the Edinburgh Whigs, under an unconstitutional regime; and one can only sympathise with him when, shut out of public life where he could excel, and kept in the backwaters of scholarship and dalliance by the Napoleonic dictatorship, he should find this backwater dominated by a female of the Napoleonic species. One hesitates, of course, to call any place that Madame de Staël inhabited a backwater. Maelstrom comes nearer to her disposition. "Storm" was his word for her (modified to *bel orage* in *Adolphe*); warming up to "earthquake" and settling finally on "volcano". And not extinct, either, like that crater to which Chateaubriand's René climbed, in a famous passage, to weep for the mere matter of an hour or two. The real Romantics were men of theatrical moments; a borrower like Constant had to endure the years. He was ten years among the explosions of Madame de Staël, and even Napoleon, it is said, could not withhold a breath of congratulation when he heard she had gone to Italy where the volcano, as he pointed out, is natural to the scenery.

Constant's own solution was simply liberal constitutionalism. Marriage, he seems to suggest, was devised by society precisely for this kind of malady, i.e. the fatigue of the imagination, the discovery that when you possessed your mistress you did not love her. Cynical—but the idea had been in his mind since he was a boy of 13. He seems to have thought that even Madame the Volcano in full eruption would become amenable after standing at the altar. He was obeying the instinct of the male who, drowning in the passion he has unwittingly roused, seeks to appease the storm by throwing off his lifebelt.

"Scène épouvantable avec Madame de Staël. J'annonce une rupture décisive. Deuxième scène. Fureur, reconciliation impossible, départ difficile. Il faut me marier."

Départ difficile—that sums up the diminuendo of human love. And even when it was not *épouvantable* it went on quietly nagging:

"Minette est de mauvaise humeur, parceque je ne veux pas veiller le soir. Il est clair que je serai forcé de me marier pour pouvoir me coucher de bonne heure."

Well, he had two good goes at it and marriage was not a success.

Adolphe is the intellectual in love, beginning it all out of *amour propre* and some fashionable imitation, creating love out of his head, rejoicing in the mind's freedom, and horrified to find that the heart desires slavery. The beauty of the book is that the theme is lived and not argued; not indeed lived with the accidental paraphernalia or even the embellishment with which life mercifully obscures fundamental human problems, but with the austere serenity of abstraction. There is a little of the Romantic foliage taken from the literature of the time—the presentiments, the solitary walks, the wintry landscape and some notes in the deathbed scene are *de rigueur*—but he is not lyrical, nor does he go back to the urbane generalities of the pure eighteenth-century manner. He is something new. The lives of the lovers are singled out like two trees in the winter, their branches articulated in exact and delicate skeleton against a clear and cloudless sky.

He was restless, it was noted. He could not keep still when he was in a room. The imagination is the most quickly wearied of our faculties; it craves for more and more stimulus. After its ecstasies it leaves a void; hollowness and listlessness lie like ashes after it has burned. Presently sentiment rewarms them and the tepid souls like Constant begin to live on the imagination's memories. They are not memories of real things; but a mistress abandoned twenty years ago begins to be clothed in a glamour which, mathematically speaking, is twice the glamour of a mistress abandoned ten years ago; and twenty times the attraction of one he happens to be living with at the moment. She, poor wretch, has to deal with him, stark naked. It is a familiar perversity. The oldest of Constant's ladies, now old enough to be his grandmother, seems almost proper for the magic state of marriageability. Alas, he had left it too late. She was dead. How far back would Constant's memories have to go before he hit upon the ultimate and assuaging woman?

At that question, out of malice to all, one wants to transplant him. One always wants to do this with the early liberals. One wants to show them where it was all leading, this exaltation of life, liberty and the pursuit of autobiography. Since that time there has been only one period in which the intellectuals have had it all their own way; when imagination and experiment were to be canonised, where liberty made its last if desiccated whoopee. One leads him into the Bloomsbury of the 'twenties. The Lawrence wave catches him, as Chateaubriand and *Corinne* caught him before. Presently he is thrown among the psycho-analysts. They seize him and one hears (as he describes the ever-enrichening associations of his memory) the inevitable question: "When did you last see your mother?" He has to confess he cannot remember: it was his father who had bothered him; *she* had died at his birth. And then one hears the shrill, scientific howl as Constant at last hears the cause of his trouble, the seat of that sullen will-lessness. It was the charm of living 130 years ago that the psychological novelists did not have to know what their own trouble was.

31

THE FIRST DETECTIVE

THE time of the year and the year itself are unknown, but one day, well before the French Revolution, a tall, good-looking, fair-haired youth was hanging about dejectedly on the quay at Ostend seeking for a boat which would take him to America. Arras was his native town, but Arras could not hold him. His energy, his vitality, his hopes demanded a larger land. Unhappily the only boats going to America were far too expensive for him, and he stood on the quay lonely, homesick and in despair. He was in this state when a stranger fell into conversation with him, a stranger who turned out to be a shipping agent and who explained that once you knew the ropes it was the simplest thing on earth to find a ship. He, personally, would see to it. The two men went off to an inn to discuss the matter further. What happened after that was never quite clear to the youth. There had been good food and drink; there appeared to have been some "dames fort aimables" whose hospitality was of "the antique kind" which did not stop at the table; he even had some recollection of being in a pleasant if rotating room and under the same eiderdown as one of the ladies. All the more astonishing therefore to wake up in the morning and find himself lying half-naked on a pile of ropes—the only ones he was to learn about—with only a couple of *écus* in his pockets. A sad story and, as the innkeeper said, he ought to be grateful that worse had not happened. But this was not the appropriate moral. The money with which Eugène-François Vidocq had planned to pay his fare to America had been stolen from his mother's baker's shop in Arras. The theft was the first major enterprise—hitherto he had only tickled pennies out of the slot in the counter with a feather dipped in glue—in a picaresque career which was to lead Eugène-François into the French, Austrian and revolutionary armies, into the perpetual company of criminals, all over the roads of France and into most of the prisons, until at last, an artist in escape and quick changes, he arrived at the Sûreté in Paris not as a convict but as its Director. To his legend as a criminal was to be added a new legend as a detective. He was to be the first of the Big Four.

The astonishing story of the life of Vidocq can be read in two French biographies, notably one by Jagot published in 1928; a far fuller and livelier account, however, is contained in the four volumes of Vidocq's own *Mémoires* published in 1829, of which, as far as I know, no complete or reliable English translation exists. A French edition in two volumes is published by the Librairie Grund. The *Mémoires* are said not to be his own work, but, whoever wrote them, the book is enormously readable, especially the opening volume. This early narrative has the rapidity, the nonchalance, the variety and crude intrigue of the good picaresque novels; and in it Vidocq is a living man and not a mere first person singular. If he touched up his own past or if someone else touched it up for him, introducing romantic coincidences—Vidocq was always running into his ex-wife, his discarded mistresses or ill-intentioned fellow prisoners, at the least desirable moments —the story gains in romance and ingenuity.

To describe Vidocq as a great criminal is inaccurate. Rather he was a reckless, adventurous young man with a gift for trouble, a true *tête brulée*. The Revolution, the war with Austria, the amateur and professional armies of the period, were his environment; the armies were recruited, dissolved, changed sides and, in default of pay, lived by their wits. Brussels was a hive of this knavery and there Vidocq found himself posing as an officer and plotting a bigamous marriage with an elderly baroness. There is some charm in his account of how his nerve went and of how he confessed to the lady. After the Ostend episode he had avoided theft and had tried to settle down with a circus. His employer tried to make him into an acrobat and failed; the alternative was the rôle of the noble savage, but he found this uncongenial, indeed terrifying: he was expected to eat birds alive and swallow stones. His next master was a wandering quack and knave who swindled farmers and who took Vidocq back to Arras, where his adventures and an orgy of forgiveness by his parents at once made him famous. Vidocq no doubt boasted. He was a great talker and something of an actor. Soon he had mistresses all over the town, was fighting duels or assaulting those who refused to fight. He found himself at last in prison.

Here one picks up the recurring pattern of Vidocq's life. Gaoled because of one woman, he intrigues with another to get him out—going this time to the length of marriage—but once he is out, the jealousy or unfaithfulness of the rescuing lady drives him again into hiding. It is a continually repeated story. Worse than his infidelity was his lack of tact. A girl called Francine, for example, risked everything to aid his escape from one gaol; yet, such was his crassness or his ill-luck, he walked straight out of the prison gates into the arms of an old mistress and unwisely spent the night with her instead of going to the woman who had rescued him. This was too much for the faithful, or at least sacrificial, Francine. It seemed to her—and to many others—that the best way to be assured of Vidocq was to get him back to prison as soon as possible. Vidocq made no pretence to virtue and delighted in the mystery which gradually grew around his character. He had the vanity of a child. Later on he was to describe with a proper sardonic agony how, when escaping from the police in Brittany and disguised as a nun, he was obliged by a farmer and his wife to occupy the same bed as their daughters, in the

34

interests of propriety. Such a trial by fire is the kind of thing picaresque literature enjoys.

The other element in the Vidocq pattern is his faculty for escape. Vidocq always held that his big conviction was unjust and that he was "framed" by a fellow prisoner. To escape was therefore a matter of justice and duty. There is something moving in this very vital man's continual struggles for liberty. The fame of his escapes eclipsed whatever other notoriety he had. At Arras the disconsolate police were driven to put out the legend that he was a werewolf. One gendarme swore that, as he laid hands on him, Vidocq turned into a bale of straw.

Awaiting trial, for example, he simply picked up the coat and helmet of the guard, which had been put on a bench near by, and walked unmolested out of court. On another occasion he locked the police up in his room. Over and over again he enjoyed the comedy of leading an unsuspecting police officer on to saying what he would do with Vidocq when he caught him. Jumping out of cabs when under escort, leaving prison by a rope at the window, sawing through manacles, digging tunnels out of gaol or making his guards drunk, became a routine. In Arras, where he was very much wanted, he lived for a year disguised as an Austrian officer and neither his family, the police nor the girl he lived with, who had known him well before, discovered his true identity.

For twelve years, while he was supposedly serving a long sentence, Vidocq was more often out of prison than in it. But it was an exhausting life; freedom was constantly menaced by blackmailing associates, and just when he seemed to have settled down happily as a draper—such was his mild ambition —he met his divorced wife and found himself keeping her and her relatives in order to shut their mouths. The worm turned. He went to the Chief of Police and made him an offer. Pardon him, leave him in peace, Vidocq said, and he

IN MY GOOD BOOKS

would help them to capture all the criminals they desired.
It cannot be said that this second period of respectable fame
makes entirely comfortable reading.   He delivered "the goods"
of course; no one could approach his abilities as a detective,
for no one else had his knowledge of the underworld.   The
vanity of criminals is as inexhaustible as their love of the great
figure; a burglar or assassin, however great in his own esteem,
was flattered if the great and mysterious Vidocq sat down with
him at the table of some shabby *marchand de vin*.   Vidocq
decoyed them with charm or effrontery, as the case demanded.
With a rather devilish gusto he will tell how, hearing So-and-so
was wanted, he would go to the house of the man's mistress,
announce her man had been caught, install himself with the
lady for a few days and (his own mistress aiding him) would
get to know the whole gang, and, at the right moment, strike.
It is a little embarrassing.   The authorities themselves became
embarrassed.   The law never feels very happy about the *agent
provocateur*.

The *Mémoires* of Vidocq are by a man who was hugely
proud of his life both as a fugitive and a pursuer of fugitives.
He had an eye for character and there are some admirable
farces of low life such as his adventures with the drunken
colonial sergeant and their riotous visits to the brothels.   The
dialogue is racy and real.   His portraits of the innumerable
"dames fort aimables" are very vivid.   He is delighted with
himself as a detective.   There is a search, at one period, for a
house where a hunchback girl lives in a quarter which at first
seems to have no hunchbacks.   Hunchbacks (Vidocq reasons)
are natural gossips—especially about other people's love affairs;
they are jealous and also very respectable.   Where do the most
respectable gossips meet?   At the milk shops.   Disguised as a
respectable man of 60 he sets out to search the most popular
creameries.   Sure enough a hunchback appears, a very Venus
of hunchbacks, of course, a great-eyed creature like a medieval

fairy. Posing as a wronged husband, Vidocq soon discovers who is living in sin in the house and so traces his victims.

One can hardly call this subtle, but the methods of Vidocq were made for the chaotic period of the Napoleonic wars and their aftermath when France swarmed with criminals. Later on, more systematic and respectable means were wanted. His day came to an end and he had the mortification of seeing another reformed criminal, his secretary, one Coco Lacour, succeed him. Coco had reformed in earnest. He had gone to the Jesuits, who made him and his wife do public penance bare-footed in the streets. A coolness existed between Vidocq and Coco. Coco was a miserable man with no air of the gentleman about him and Vidocq had pointed out that a touch more polish in his conversation as a member of the Big Four would be an advantage. (After all, Vidocq had very nearly married a baroness, a Belgian baroness it is true, but still . . .) Coco resented his lessons in etiquette. Vidocq, in his jealousy, has drawn a very funny portrait of the little reformed sinner sitting all day by the Pont Neuf fishing while, at home, his wife is doing a good trade in clothes with prostitutes.

Once out of favour Vidocq is said to have faked a robbery and then to have made arrests to show how clever he was; but the trick was discovered and the words *agent provocateur* finally doomed him. He started a paper factory which failed, a detective agency which declined into triviality. He died at last in poverty. There is one sentence in the *Mèmoires* which I like to think he really wrote:

Les voleurs de profession (it says) sont tous ceux qui volontairement ou non, ont contracté l'habitude de s'approprier le bien d'autrui.

GERMINAL

I n the portrayal of character for its own sake and of the sociable rather than the social man, the English novelists have always excelled. The social man, the creature of ideas who must sacrifice some of his idiosyncrasy to environment, movements or theories, appears in a few exceptional books, books like *The Pilgrim's Progress*, *Gulliver*, *Jonathan Wild* and later on in *Hard Times* and *The Way of All Flesh*. Elsewhere he is to be found mostly in the background. There is emotion about society (Dickens), but there is repugnance to ideas about it. It is remarkable how little the English novel was influenced in the nineteenth century by the political and scientific thought of the time, though some passages in George Eliot and Mrs. Gaskell show the novelist dealing with concrete event. Vainly we look, for example, for any sign that Darwin had been read, at any rate with an eye to the reconsideration of society. Thomas Hardy merely changes the pronoun by which one usually addresses the Deity; and at the turn of the century, Arnold Bennett performs a typical feat in importing the methods of the French naturalists, and leaving out the whole philosophical and political impulse behind that movement. This repugnance is supposed to have changed now. Yet so blankly do the alternatives of sociability and society present themselves to the English novelist that Wells thought he had to abandon character altogether. Since then there has been a good deal of talk about Marx and social realism which may be fruitful but which so far has produced next to nothing in the novel. Why, I am not sure; perhaps because we left learning about the nineteenth century too late.

38

How late may be seen by reading Zola's *Germinal*. It was published in 1885. I do not know whether Zola ever read Marx, though I believe that at this time he certainly had not—but he had heard of the First International; he knew the doctrines of Anarchism and its personalities; he had read Darwin. He was familiar with those Siamese twins, the idea of the struggle for life and the struggle of the classes, contests so congenial to his dramatic temperament. He saw not indeed the grey trudge of economic man, but, more picturesquely and not a little mystically—mouths. Mouths wide open, groups of mouths, kinds of mouths; for his curiously divided personality the vision became an orgy of gluttony both gross and idealised. ("Seed" and "gluttony" are the recurring keywords of *Germinal*.) Where is the English parallel to the bad dream of *Germinal*? There is none. The religious conscience of the English novelists was certainly troubled by Darwin, their social conscience not at all. The fittest, the English middle-classes and their writers seem to have assumed, had survived.

And, to be more particular, we not only had Darwin but we had the mines. Where still is the English *Germinal*? There have been English novels about the coal-mines in the last twenty years, novels concerned with the social question. There have even been talent, experience, feeling. What has been lacking? Genius, except in the abortive case of D. H. Lawrence, of course; but above all a philosophy of life which could feed the kind of genius this novel calls for. Zola dug out of nineteenth-century speculation a theatrical but also profound view of mankind. He had temperament, will and curiosity. And he had the chronic ability to write novels on a variety of very different subjects. All these qualities the English mining novelists lack.

Comparing their books with *Germinal* one sees at once that they suffer also from a fatal moral simplicity. There is the choke of the hard-luck story in their throats. And from their chief fallacy Zola is entirely free: the fallacy that people who are starved, poor and oppressed are good and noble because they are poor and oppressed. And he is also free of the rider to the fallacy: that their sufferings and struggles make them more virtuous. Zola's drawing undoubtedly exaggerated—temperament *is* exaggeration—and in the way which his period tended to exaggerate. His inverted idealism idealised the monstrous. But his nineteenth-century preoccupation with corruption and nightmare did show him that poverty may lead to degradation, that souls may become exhausted, that the moral victories of poverty may be at the cost of humanity itself. This was not, it is true, Zola's final judgment. He appears in *Germinal* to back the *bête humaine*, and to admire the brute mob because they are bestial and brutal, or rather, because he sees in them a force of nature which is overthrowing, on Darwinian lines, the weaklier types and eventually transcending them. The miners are the seed sown in the horror of the dark earth and will one day germinate and rise through the mud to free themselves and the world. So there are positive and negative poles to Zola's philosophy. In the English novels on the subject there is no similar organic conception of the nature of men. They are not tragic figures because they are never struggling with themselves. What miner in an English novel ever misbehaved, unless he was a blackleg or a labelled villain? True, he may drink or fight a bit, but that is merely toughness. He never has evil in his nature. Zola's central character and hero bashes a man's brains out. He does this because of an hereditary poison on his soul. One smiles at Zola's topical little fuss about heredity, but the case shows the difference between the pieties of the political Sunday School and the freedom of imaginative literature.

The two great things in the main outline of *Germinal* are its romantic grasp of the scene—the sustained symbolism—and the handling of groups of people. As he approaches it at night through the freezing gale, the mine appears to Etienne first of all as two points of yellow light like the eyes of a night animal; then its dragon-like form takes shape, the gasp of steam from its engine is like a monster's breathing. The monster squats on the plain; the cages whirr down full of men; up comes the coal; the mine is a monster devouring men, excreting coal. That sombre opening character is unforgettable. One is overpowered and frightened. What a relief to meet the sardonic old night-watchman, Bonnemort, the first character, the old man whom the mine cannot kill; and then how brilliant of Zola, a master of the strategy of story-telling, to show us that the relief we found in Bonnemort is deceptive. His is no sunny face to charm the visitor with; he is—the malice of the mine itself, the shrewd grin that remains on life when it is maimed. There are the gluttony of that animal the mine, the gluttony of those animals the Hennebeaus, the owning family with their terrible, overfed daughter; and this is set against the gluttony of the miners which is very different: the rabid gluttony of the starved. Zola's poetic symbolism no doubt gets out of hand at times, especially later on when the shouting mouths of the rioters are caught by the red light of the setting sun and seem to be blotched with guzzled blood. That is a bad moment; the fresco becomes as false as a poster; but, in general, the romanticism of Zola transfigures the enormous dossier which he collected. At the end, in that terrifying chapter where the underground landslides make the mine cave in, so that the monster, which has devoured so many, is itself devoured, the preposterous symbolism comes off because Zola has prepared the way with extraordinary technical thoroughness. The engine goes:

> And then a terrible thing was seen; the engine, dislocated from its massive foundation, with broken limbs was struggling against death; it moved; it straightened its crank, its giant's knee, as though to rise: but crushed and swallowed up, it was dying.

"Its crank, its giant's knee"—fact and symbol continue their fertile marriage to the end.

Too much nightmare, it has been said. Yes, but it is a nightmare of fact not of mere eloquence. Still it must be admitted that *Germinal* destroys one's capacity to feel. At least it does that to mine. Each agony wrings the neck of its predecessor. One is broken at the end, not by feeling, but by the unremittingly documented thunderclaps of the drama. Strangely enough it is the briefly drawn soldiers, rather than the miners, who move one most. This may be because they are silent; or simply because Zola with his genius for getting the feeling of groups of people, has got their essential passive pathos. Then that copulation! The mines appear like an erotic gymnasium, and it gets a bit dubious after the first two or three hundred acts of rutting, though Zola's invariable note of the positions adopted by lovers is as professionally pernicketty as Casanova's and is a relief after Lawrence. (Is this realism or mania? Zola's personal anxiety about impotence?) And what a lot of dangling breasts and posturing bottoms!

The real stuff of *Germinal* is the documentation and the groups of people on which the nightmare throws its strange light. This most bourgeois of all the bourgeois gave himself six months to get up the facts for *Germinal*; in that time he seems to have assimilated not merely all the technical, economic and social details of mining—see, for example, his knowledge of the structure of the pit-shaft, which becomes important in that terrific chapter when Souvarine, the anarchist, goes down alone by the ladder to saw through the beams and wreck the mine—but to have fertilised them so that they are no longer dead stuff in a notebook, but life. I do not know whether it is a defect of our novels about mining that they are written by ex-miners. Zola, who came from outside, surpasses them, perhaps because what is thoroughly and consciously conquered by force of will is enormously stimulating to invention. The fault of the modern novelist in general is that he does not go outside his own world for his material and I think that the decline of the power to tell a story or of the interest in doing so is due to this. Zola is an example of the value of pure curiosity. It is said that he had no natural power of observation; he relied upon learned facts, and when a piece of observation is put in to clinch a picture—the woman bringing her children to enjoy the sight of the riot, another woman stopping and re-starting her work at the sink while she quarrels, so that potato peeling goes on half the morning, the soldier blinking just before he is provoked to fire at the crowd, the comical formal politeness of the Mde. Raisseneur, a real tricoteuse, as she agrees with Souvarine's bloodiest theories—it is wonderful in its effect because it is exact. Zola's ability to describe the movements of crowds is due to the fact that, unlike natural observers, he had to study crowds like a statistician and is therefore not carried away. Timid and plump, fussing with pencil and paper, Zola stands on the outskirts, noting not only the leaf-like swirl of humanity, but those single eddies, those sudden arrivals and departures of individuals, which indicate more than anything the pulse of a crowd's unreason.

One Zola believed that evil existed in all men and also that man was an amoral natural force; another Zola—the plump little professor with a halo in Forain's funny caricature—believed in man's ideal aims. This duality enables him to make the agitator, Etienne, a complete human being. *Germinal* can be read as the case against the miners as well as the case for them and, looking at Etienne, you can say on the evidence, either that here is a man exploiting the workers in his own ambition to get out of the working class; or here is an idealist who, though he sacrifices the workers in fact, is in effect leading them to their emancipation. Working-class leaders are not commonly studied with Zola's candour; they are never presented as egotists unless the novelist's object is to denounce them.

43

Of course, one may read *Germinal* and think that its philosophical background is as dated as the bestial conditions it describes; the mines are no longer brothels; people no longer starve at work; they starve for lack of it. War has become the crux of the social problem. But the greatness of *Germinal* lies in the exalted thoroughness of its exposure of the situation as it was during Zola's time, and equally in the mastery of its story. Its lesson to English novelists is that their education is incomplete and sterile if it does not apply itself to reinterpreting contemporary history.

SOFA AND CHEROOT

WHEN we ask ourselves what the heroes of novels did with themselves in their spare time, a hundred to a hundred and fifty years ago, there can be no hesitation in the answer. Novel after novel confirms it, from *Tom Brown at Oxford* back to Fielding and Smollett: they stretched themselves on a sofa, lit a cheroot and picked up again *The Adventures of Gil Blas*. Once more they were on the road with that hopeful young valet from the Asturias as he went from town to town in Old Castile in the reign of Philip IV, always involved in the love affairs and the money secrets of his employers, until, a model of Self-Help, he enters the valet-keeping classes himself and becomes secretary to the Prime Minister. Say your prayers (his loving parents advised him when he set out for the University of Salamanca which he never reached, at least not to become a student), avoid bad company, and above all keep your fingers out of other people's property. Gil Blas ignored this good advice from the beginning and returned home at last to a benign retirement as a rich man and a noble. Not exactly a sinner, not exactly virtuous, Gil Blas is a kind of public statue to what we would call the main chance and to what the Spaniards call *conformidad* or accepting the world for what it is and being no better than your neighbour.

English taste has always been responsive to Le Sage; his influence on English writers and his vogue were far greater among us than they were in France. Defoe probably read him; Smollett translated and copied him. Le Sage became the intermediary between ourselves and that raw, farcical, sour, bitter picaresque literature of Spain which, for some reason, has always taken the English fancy. Gil Blas took the strong meat of the rogues' tales and made it palatable for us. He put a few clothes on the awful, goose-fleshed and pimpled carnality of Spanish realism, disguised starvation as commercial anxiety, filled the coarse vacuum, which the blatant passions of the Spaniards create around them, with the rustle and crackle of intrigue. We who live in the north feel that no man has the right to be so utterly stripped of illusions as the Spaniard seems to be; Gil Blas covered that blank and too virile nakedness, not indeed with illusions, but with a degree of elegance. It was necessary. For though the picaresque novel appealed to that practical, empirical, rule-of-thumb strain in the English mind, to that strong instinct of sympathy we have for an ingenious success story—and all picaresque novels are really unholy success stories—we have not the nervous system to stand some of the things the Spaniards can stand. What is *Lazarillo de Tormes*, the most famous of the picaresque novels, but the subject of starvation treated as farce? We could never make jokes about starvation.

Compared to the real Spanish thing, *Gil Blas* is a concoction which lacks the native vividness. It belongs to the middle period of picaresque literature when the rogue has become a good deal of the puritan. Historically this transition is extraordinarily interesting. One could not have a clearer example of the way in which the form and matter of literature are gradually fashioned by economic change in society. The literature of roguery which Le Sage burgled for the compilation of *Gil Blas* is the fruit of that economic anarchy which early capitalism introduced into Spanish life. In England the typical character of the period is the puritan; in Spain his opposite number is the man who has to live by his wits. A system has broken down, amid imperialist war and civil revolt, poverty has become general among those who rely on honest labour. There is only one way for the energetic to get their living.

46

They can rush to the cities and especially to the Court and help themselves to the conquered wealth of the New World, to that wealth or new money which has brought poverty to the rest of the population by destroying the value of the old money. I am not sure how far economists would confirm the generalisation, but it seems that Spain used foreign conquest and the gold of the New World to stave off the introduction of private capitalism, and the parallel with Nazi policy is close. At any rate, instead of the successful trader, Spain produces the trader frustrated, in other words, the rogue.

They are, of course, both aspects of the same kind of man, and that is one of the reasons why Defoe and English literature got so much out of the picaresque novel, so that it is hard to distinguish between Defoe's diligent nonconformists and his ingenious cheats and gold-diggers. Gil Blas himself represents the mingling of the types. He is not many hours on the road before he is adroitly flattered and cheated. It is the first lesson of the young and trusting go-getter in the ways of the world. Until he gets to Madrid his career is one long list of disasters. He is captured by robbers, robbed by cocottes in the jewel racket. The hopeful young man on the road to an estimable career at the university is soon nothing but a beggar and is well on the way to becoming a knave by the time he sets up in partnership with a provincial quack doctor. Madrid really saves him from the louder kinds of crime. Intrigue is, he learns, far more remunerative. He goes from one household to another as a valet, filling his pockets as he goes. The knave has given place to the young man with an eye for a good situation and whose chief social ambition is to become a *señorito* or *petit maître*, extravagantly dressed and practising the gaudy manners of the innumerable imitators of the aristocracy. No one is more the new bourgeois than Gil Blas—especially in his great scorn for the bourgeois. And there is something very oily about him. How careful he is to worm his way into his master's confidence so that he may become a secretary and rake off small commissions or in the hope that he will be left something in the old man's will! Much later, by his attention to duty, he becomes a secretary to a Minister, and sells offices and pockets bribes. What of it?—he is no worse, he says, than the Minister himself, or the heir to the throne who has dirty money dealings all round, or those old ladies who pose as aristocrats in order to palm off their daughters on wealthy lovers. There is a sentence describing an old actress which puts Gil Blas's ambition in a nutshell. She was

> Une de ces héroïnes de galanterie qui savent plaire jusque dans leur vieillesse et qui meurent chargées des depouilles de deux ou trois générations.

"To be loaded with the spoils"—that is very different from the fate of the real *picaro* of the earlier dispensation, and Gil Blas is not entirely cynical about it. "After all" (he seems to say, his eyes sharp with that frantic anxiety which still exercises Spaniards when there is a question of money), "after all, I worked for it, didn't I? I served my master's interest? I'm a *sort* of honest man." And when he decides to keep a valet of his own and interviews the applicants, there is a charm in the way he rejects the one who has a pious face and picks out one who has been a bit of a twister too.

The character of Gil Blas himself could hardly be the attraction of Le Sage's book, and indeed he is little more than a lay figure. The pleasures of picaresque literature are like the pleasures of travel. There is continuous movement, variety of people, change of scene. The assumption that secret self-interest, secret passions, are the main motives in human conduct does not enlarge the sensibility—Le Sage came before the sensibility of the eighteenth century awakened—but it sharpens the wits, fertilises invention and enlarges gaiety. But again, the book is poor in individual characters. One must get out of one's head all expectation of a gallery of living portraits. Le Sage belonged to the earlier tradition of Molière and Jonson and foreshadowed creations like Jonathan Wild: his people are types, endeared to us because they are familiar and perennial. You get the quack, the quarrelling doctors fighting over the body of the patient, the efficient robber, the impotent old man and his young mistress, the blue-stocking, the elderly virgin on the verge of wantonness, the man of honour, the jealous man, the poet, the actress, the courtier. Each is presented vivaciously, with an eye for self-deception and the bizarre. The story of the Bishop of Granada has become the proverbial fable of the vanity of authors. And that scene in the Escorial when the Prime Minister, in order to impress the King and the Court, takes his secretary and papers out into the garden and pretends to be dictating though he is really gossiping, is delicious debunking of that rising type—the great business man.

The pleasure of *Gil Blas* is that it just goes on and on in that clear, exact, flowing style which assimilates the sordid, the worldly, or the fantastic romance with easy precision, unstrained and unperturbed. It is the pleasure of the perfect echo, the echo of a whole literature and of a period. You are usually smiling, sometimes you even laugh out loud; then boredom comes as one incident clutches the heels of another and drags it down. No one can read the novel of adventure for adventure's sake to the end; and yet, put *Gil Blas* down for a while, and you take it up again. It is like a drug. Self-interest, the dry eye, the low opinion, the changing scene, the ingenuity of success, the hard grin of the man of the world— those touch something in our natures which, for all our romanticism and our idealism, have a weakness for the *modus vivendi*. The puritan and the rogue join hands.

49

A RUSSIAN BYRON

MIKHAIL YUREVICH LERMONTOFF was born in the year before Waterloo and was killed in a duel twenty-seven years later, a year after the publication of the novel which brought him fame throughout Europe. The extraordinary duel in the last chapter but one of *A Hero of Our Own Times* is said to have been exactly prophetic of the manner of his death. Lermontoff had declared through his chief character that life was a bad imitation of a book; and the episode, if true, looks like some carefully planned Byronic legend.

A Hero of Our Own Times belongs to that small and elect group of novels which portray a great typical character who resumes the fashion and idiosyncrasy of a generation. Pechorin, the "hero", is consciously a Russian Byron. He is cold, sensual, egoistical, elegant. He is neurotic, bored and doomed. Only one passion is unexhausted—and this is the making of him—the passion for personal freedom. He is the cold, experimental amorist celebrated by Pushkin (I quote from Oliver Elton's translation of *Eugeny Onegin*):

> Men once extolled cold-blooded raking
> As the true science of love-making:
> Your own trump everywhere you blew . . .
> Such grave and serious recreation
> Beseemed old monkeys, of those days. . . .

Pechorin becomes the slave of perpetual travel, and finally fulfils himself not in love but in action. Byron goes to Greece. Pechorin becomes the soldier of the Caucasus who plays with life and death. He drives himself to the limit, whether it is

in the duel on the edge of the precipice down which his absurd
rival in love is thrown; or in the dramatic bet with Vulich
where he draws a revolver and puts sixty roubles on the doctrine
of predestination; or in the final episode when he goes in
alone to collar the Cossack who has run amok. In its greater
actors the Byronic pose of weariness is balanced by love of
living dangerously in action, and here it is interesting to contrast the character of Constant's Adolphe with a man like
Pechorin. Adolphe also is the imaginative man who loves
from the head and then revenges himself secretively and cruelly
upon the strong-minded woman who is devouring him and
with whom he is afraid to break: Pechorin, more histrionic and
less sensitive (more Byronic, in short), loves from the head
also but takes special care to avoid strong-minded women. He
possesses, but is not possessed. He prefers the weak and yielding who respond at once to cruelty and whom he can abandon
quickly. Faced with the strong-minded, Pechorin becomes a
man of action and makes his getaway. Readers of *A Hero
of Our Own Times* will remember how Pechorin dealt with
the determined duplicity of Taman, the smuggler's girl, when
she took him out in her boat on a moonlight night. He threw
her into the sea. What would not Adolphe have given for
such decisiveness? What would he not have given for that
Byronic ruthlessness in action, who knew only the cool vacilla-
tions of the mind? Of the two characters, Pechorin's is the
more arrested and adolescent. He has not Adolphe's sensibility to the tragedy of the imagination. He does not suffer.
Pechorin is sometimes a 17-year-old sentimentalist who blames
the world:

> I have entered upon this life when I have already lived
> it in imagination, with the result that it has become tedious
> and vile to me. I am like a man who has been reading
> the bad imitation of a book with which he has been long
> familiar.

But perhaps the main difference between these lovers of freedom
is merely one of age after all. Pechorin-Lermontoff is young:
Adolphe is the creation of an older man. Pechorin says:

> Now I only want to be loved, and that by a very few
> women. Sometimes (terrible thought) I feel as if a lasting
> tie would satisfy me.

Adolphe would have been incapable of this naïve Byronic
jauntiness; but he would have raised a sympathetic eyebrow
at that first hint of nostalgia for respectable marriage.

This was not a solution which Russian literature was yet
to permit its Pechorins. Press on to the middle of the century
and we find Turgenev's Rudin, all Byronism spent, and with
no exciting war of Russian Imperialism to occupy him, conducting an affair as heartless and disgraceful as Pechorin's
affair with Princess Mary and very similar to it. But Rudin
is reduced to the condition of an unheroic, rootless talker
with no corresponding performance. Byronism with its roots
in the Napoleonic wars, was a fashion which fortunately could
give the best of its followers something to do. For the mal-
adjusted and the doomed there were duels; even better there
was always a war and the cause of Liberty. The poseur of
Venice attained some dignity at Missolonghi: and the sentimentalist of the Caucasus, reviving new trouble with an old
mistress, and in the midst of the old trouble with a new one,
could feel the heady contagion of that half-savage passion for
freedom with which his enemies, the Tartar tribesmen, were
imbued.

Travel is one of the great rivals of women. The officers
and visitors at the garrison town of Narzan spend their time
drinking the waters, making love, scandal-mongering and playing cards; and into this gossiping frontier outpost Pechorin
brings something like the preposterous coldness, austerity and
violence of the mountain scene outside the town. The coach

arrives, he yawns, stays a night, throws his diaries to a friend in lieu of a renewal of friendship and drives on, another Childe Harold on an eternal Grand Tour of the battle fronts. The *Hero* is not one of the calculated, constructed, and balanced books of maturity; its virtues and defects are all of youth. The book appears to pour out of the Caucasus itself. It is one of those Romantic novels in which a place and not a woman has suddenly crystallised a writer's experience and called out all his gifts. "I was posting from Tiflis"—that opening sentence of Lermontoff's classically nonchalant prose, takes the heart a stride forward at once. Like the traveller, we step out of ourselves into a new world. True, it is the fashionable step back to Rousseau, for the *Hero* is nothing if not modish; but who does not feel again with Lermontoff, as he gazes at the ravines, breathes the rare, crisp, savage air and sees the golden dawn on the upper snows, who does not feel the force of the Romantic emotion? "When we get close to Nature the soul sheds all that it has artificially acquired to be what it was in its prime and probably will be again some day." One is captivated by such a nostalgia, by its youthful and natural idealism and by the artifice of its youthful melancholy.

The structure of the book is both ingenious and careless. Later novelists would have been tempted to a full-length portrait of Pechorin. Lermontoff is episodic yet tells us all we need to know in a handful of exciting short stories. We first hear of Pechorin at two removes. The narrator meets a curt, humdrum officer who has known him and who tells the first story of Pechorin's capture and abandonment of Bela, the Tartar girl. Passion has ended in boredom. In the next episode, when Pechorin meets again the officer who had helped him fight the girl's murderers, one sees the Byronic mask go up at the mere hint of the "incident". After that Pechorin himself describes his adventures in his diaries. They tell, with sadistic detachment, of how he is playing with the despair of

an old mistress while planning to convert another woman's
fear and hatred of him to love.   He succeeds.   Which is all
Pechorin wants—a victory for his vanity.   He explains this
quite candidly to her.   And he is candid not because he is
an honest man but because, of course, he is interested only in
himself.   Equally coolly, he plans that the duel he fights with
her lover shall take place on the famous precipice.

   Pechorin's notions are not merely the melodramatic.   He is
the enemy of simple, highfalutin romanticism; his taste is for
the reserved, the complex and mysterious.   The precipice is
chosen, for example, as a masterpiece of vengeance, because he
has discovered that his opponent intends to fool him with
blank cartridges.   The opposing faction at Narzan has perceived that Pechorin's vulnerable point is his pride; knock the
Byronic mask off his face and there will stand an empty actor.
Lermontoff is an expert in subtleties like this.   In the final
episode, when Vulich, the gambler, proposes to discover whether
he is or is not fated to die that day, by putting a revolver to
his head and pulling the trigger, the suicide is abortive.   But
Vulich does die that day, and in a most unexpected manner.
The Calvinist doctrine of predestination in Byron's Aberdeen
has become the almost exotic Oriental Kismet in Lermontoff's
Caucasus.

   To the modern novelist, tired of the many and overdone
conventions of the novel, the apparently loose and unconnected
construction of *A Hero of Our Times* offers a suggestion.
Lermontoff's method is to thread together a string of short
stories about a central character, using an inside and an outside
point of view.   But before he did this Lermontoff had decided
what were the important things in Pechorin's character   They
were, as it happened, all aspects of Byronism.   Mr. Desmond
MacCarthy has said in an essay on Pushkin, that from Byron
and Pushkin "men caught the infection of being defiantly
themselves"; in so planning, however, they became other than

themselves. They invented a simplified *persona*. It is this simplification of Pechorin's character which is exciting. The detailed realism of the modern novel tells us far too much, without defining the little that it is absolutely essential to know. In what modern novels are the main traits of a hero of *our* own times delineated? It is the measure of the failure of modern novelists that they have not observed and defined a characteristic man of these years; and the explanation of the failure is our lack of moral and political perceptiveness. Our novels would be shorter, more readable and more important if we had one or two more ideas about our times and far fewer characters.

A COMIC NOVEL

THE modern novel has reached such a pitch of competence and shapeliness, that we are shocked at the disorderliness of the masterpieces. In the modern novel we are looking at a neatly barbered suburban garden; in the standard works how often do we have the impression of bowling through the magnificent gateway of a demesne only to find the house and gardens are unfinished or are patched up anyhow, as if the owner had tired of his money in the first few weeks and after that had passed his life in a daydream of projects for ever put off. We feel the force of a great power which is never entirely spent, but which cannot be bothered to fulfil itself. In short, we are up against the carelessness, the lethargy, the enormous bad taste of genius, its liability to accident, its slovenly and majestic conceit that anything will do. *Don Quixote* falls in half, the *Chartreuse* and *Le Rouge et le Noir* go shockingly to pieces, Tolstoy stuffs a history book into *War and Peace*, Fielding and Dickens pad and Dostoevski wanders into ideological journalism. And then there is *Dead Souls*. You reach the second part of that masterpiece to find the editor's maddening note over and over again in the text: "Here a hiatus occurs in the manuscript." Worse, you discover that Gogol burned the manuscript of the last part and that the full story of Chichikov, the swindler, will never be known.

Perhaps it is as well that Gogol could not pull himself together for this second plunge. The remorse of comedians is painful, and it is pitiable to see an artist rounding upon his art or mistaking his ethical impulses for his artistic ones. The kind of virtue which has been successfully fought off until

middle age is apt at that time to have its dull, industrious
revenge if it has been fought too hard in youth. Given the
choice, it would, ideally, be better for an artist to let his egotism
drive him to madness as Goya's did, than for it to become
apostolic. For all we know, therefore, we should be grateful
that the second part of *Dead Souls* was not completed. The loss
may mean something on the same noble level as the second part
of *Quixote*, but we know that Gogol was worried about his
humour and that he was planning to put everything right by
following the model of the *Divine Comedy*! We could perhaps
pin some hope on the fabulous medieval and heroic side to
Gogol's genius—the tremendous story of *Taras Bulba* is the pre-
eminent example of this vein; but knowing the curious guilt
which ate into the latter part of Gogol's life and the peculiarities
of his conversion at the hands of a contemporary Rasputin,
it looks as though the starch of religiosity was stiffening him.

"Dead Souls—no, I'll never allow such a thing", said the
Russian censor, "our soul is immortal; there is no dead soul;
the author rises against immortality." (See Janko Lavrin's
useful little book on *Gogol* published fifteen years ago.) The
title *is* misleading. We have had a good deal of the Russian
soul in our time and the idea of a dead Russian soul is doubly
sombre. I wonder how many people have put the book back
on the library shelf without realising that they were rejecting
one of the world's great comic novels. Chichikov is not, I
think, a comic character to be compared with Pickwick or
Don Quixote—he belongs rather to the line of Gil Blas, to
those whose antics spring from self-interest and not from the
follies of the heart. But Chichikov is a superb comic device.
The originality and farce of the idea which animates him take
the breath away. One is paralysed by humorous expectation.
Chichikov is any carpet-bagger, any bucket-shop proprietor, any
prosaic commercial traveller of distressingly commonplace
ambitions, whose gift of the gab is given an extra flight by

Gogol's gift of fantasy. As a fraud Chichikov is mousey, but he understands the lower side of human nature and that one of the quickest ways to the human heart is to offer it something for nothing.

It is pleasant to roll his simple scheme over the tongue again. Since the previous census in which every landowner had to give a list of the serfs or "Souls" on his estate and on whom he had to pay head tax, a number would have died. The landowner still had to pay the tax until the next census. Why not therefore (Chichikov argued) offer to buy these dead names —for that is all they were—pay the taxes himself, and then, taking the title deeds to a bank, pose as the owner of so many thousand serfs, raise a large mortgage on an apparently thriving estate, and make a rich marriage? For a novelist one cannot imagine a more useful device for collecting a variety of human character, for farcical interviews, for spying into strange interiors and the uncovering of stranger motives. Chichikov's scheme was a passport to the whole of Russia. As a servant, Gil Blas became an expert on the habits of the Spanish aristocracy and the demi-monde; as a buffoon and victim Pickwick travelled through England; as a disinterested lunatic and comic martyr Don Quixote travelled Spain. They are all the tools of circumstance, clowns who get slapped and come to grief. But Chichikov succeeds or almost succeeds. In chapter after chapter, he is the master of every situation. The clowns are his victims. Even when disaster temporarily singes him at N—— where he has triumphed for so long, we know that he will soon cook up something new. Puzzled at first by his dimness as a person, we perceive that his deadly seriousness and touchy anxiety about his scheme are in themselves comical. He is astonished when people hesitate to take the bait. The bluffer believes in his own bluff. He has, what we often observe, the fundamental stupidity of the over-ingenious and too original mind.

Novels which have been fitted to an idea, usually run to the artifices of the theatre, and there is more than a note or two from the Molière farces in Gogol's situations. In his work as a playwright Gogol in fact followed Molière, and scene after scene in *Dead Souls* would have been pounced upon by the dramatist. Take the interview with Sobakevitch, the great hairy, cunning, and bear-like man who haggles over kopecks as if he were in an Eastern *souk*. Sobakevitch seeks to put up the price of his dead serfs by saying what a wonderful blacksmith or what a brilliant saddler, poor So-and-so was. He must be worth an extra five roubles because he was a good workman. The unexpected capping of one absurd situation with another in this fashion is pure theatre. The interview with the stupid widow who is eager to sell but who suspects all the time she is being swindled and tries hard to palm off lard or corn instead, has the same theatrical quality. Gogol has seized upon the stage value of a character who is so obstinate and suspicious that she can only go on repeating the same fixed idea. Her "What troubles me is the fact that they are dead" is another: "Mais qu'est ce qu'il fait dans cette galère?"

"In everything the will of God, madam," said Chichikov with a sigh. "Against the divine wisdom it is not for us to rebel. Pray hand them over to me, Natasia Petrovna."

"Hand over whom?"

"The dead peasants."

"But how could I do that?"

"Quite simply. Sell them to me, and I will give you some money in exchange."

"But how am I to sell them to you? I scarcely understand what you mean. Am I to dig them up again from the ground?"

Chichikov perceived that the old lady was altogether at sea, and that he must explain the matter; wherefore in a few words he informed her that the transfer or purchase

of the souls in question would take place merely on paper—
that the said souls would be listed as still alive.

"And what good would they be to you?" asked his hostess,
staring at him with her eyes distended.

"That is *my* affair."

"But they are *dead* souls."

"Who said they were not? The mere fact of their being
dead entails upon you a loss as dead as the souls, for you
have to continue paying the tax upon them, whereas *my*
plan is to relieve you both of the tax and of the resultant
trouble. *Now* do you understand? And I will not only
do as I say but also hand you over fifteen roubles per soul.
Is that clear enough?"

"Yes—but I do not know," said his hostess diffidently.
"You see, never before have I sold dead souls."

"Quite so. It would be a surprising thing if you had.
But surely you do not think that these dead souls are in
the least worth keeping?"

"Oh no, indeed! Why should they be worth keeping?
I am sure they are not so. The only thing which troubles
me is the fact that they are *dead*."

"She seems a truly obstinate old woman!" was Chichikov's
inward comment. "Look here, madam," he added aloud.
"You reason well, but you are simply ruining yourself by
continuing to pay the tax upon dead souls as though they
were still alive."

"Oh, good sir, do not speak of it!" the lady exclaimed.
"Three weeks ago I took a hundred and fifty roubles to
the Assessor, and buttered him up, and——"

"Then you see how it is, do you not? Remember that,
according to my plan, you will never again have to butter
up the Assessor, seeing that it will be I who will be paying
for those peasants—I, not *you*, for I shall have taken
over the dues upon them, and have transferred them to
myself as so many *bona fide* serfs. Do you understand *at
last*?"

However, the old lady still communed with herself. She

could see that the transaction would be to her advantage, yet it was one of such a novel and unprecedented nature that she was beginning to fear lest this purchaser of souls intended to cheat her. Certainly he had come from God only knew where, and at the dead of night, too!

"Let us shake hands over it," advised Chichikov.

"But, sir, I have never in my life sold dead folk—only living ones. Three years ago I transferred two wenches to Protopopov for a hundred roubles apiece, and he thanked me kindly, for they turned out splendid workers—able to make napkins or anything else."

"Yes, but with the living we have nothing to do, damn it! I am asking you only about *dead* folk."

"Yes, yes, of course. But at first sight I felt afraid lest I should be incurring a loss—lest you should be wishing to outwit me, good sir. You see, the dead souls are worth rather more than you have offered for them."

"See here, madam. (What a woman it is!) *How* could they be worth more? Think for yourself. They are so much loss to you—so much loss, do you understand? Take any worthless, rubbishly article you like—a piece of old rag, for example. That rag will yet fetch its price, for it can be bought for paper-making. But these dead souls are good for *nothing at all*. Can you name anything that they *are* good for?"

"True, true—they *are* good for nothing. But what troubles me is the fact that they are dead."

"What a blockhead of a creature!" said Chichikov to himself, for he was beginning to lose patience. "Bless her heart, I may as well be going. She has thrown me into a perfect sweat, the cursed old shrew!"

In the main—and here it is like *Gil Blas* again—*Dead Souls* is a collection of genre portraits; it is a sort of provincial social anatomy of Russia based on universal types—the foolish credulous couple whose kisses are so long that you "could smoke a small cigar before they had finished"; the town liar, the gambler, the drunkard, the miser, the crafty man, the jack-in-office, the settled official and the soldier.

The difference between farce and humour in literature is, I suppose, that farce strums louder and louder on one string, while humour varies its note, changes its key, grows and spreads and deepens until it may indeed reach tragic depths. Gogol's humour has not only the eye for the comic particularity, the ridiculous situation, but is based on a genius for humorous generalising. His generalisations are not facetious nor strained. They convey not fantastifications of life, but the full easy feeling of life itself, as though his humour was its breath, blood and natural condition and not a spectator's witty convulsions. Gogol's gallery is short of women to whom he was in life little attached; but this lack of experience or distaste for the subject is turned very cunningly to advantage by his generalising faculty. He is describing the ladies of N——:

> . . . I should need to say a great deal about the ladies themselves and to describe in most vivid of colours their social intercourse and spiritual qualities. Yet this would be a difficult thing for me to do since, on the one hand, I should be hampered by my boundless respect for the women-folk of all Civil Service officials, and, on the other hand— well, simply by the innate arduousness of the task. The ladies of N—— were —— But no, I cannot do it. My heart has already failed me. Come, come! The ladies of N—— were distinguished for —— But it's no use; somehow my pen seems to refuse to move over the paper— it seems to be weighted as with a plummet of lead. Very well. That being so I will merely say a word or two concerning the most prominent tints of the feminine pallette of N—— merely a word or two concerning the outward appearance of its ladies. . . . The ladies of N—— were pre-eminently "presentable".

And further on:

> In addition, I may say, like most of the female world of

St. Petersburg, the ladies of N—— were careful and refined in their choice of words and phrases. Never did a lady say "I blew my nose", or "I perspired", or "I spat". No, it had to be "I relieved my nose through the expedient of wiping it with my handkerchief" and so forth. Again, to say "This glass, or this plate, smells badly" was forbidden. Rather, the proper phrase in such a case was "This glass, or this plate, is not behaving very well"—or some such formula. In fact, to refine the Russian tongue the more thoroughly something like half the words in it were cut out: which circumstance necessitated very frequent recourse to the tongue of France, since the same words, if spoken in French, were another matter altogether, and one could use even blunter ones than the ones originally objected to.

(This is from D. J. Hogarth's translation in *Everyman*: Mrs. Garnett's rendering, which I have not by me as I write, is, I remember, far more spirited and fluent.) Gogol's generalisations, which link up the points of action, are never flat; some touch in them, like the comic personal reluctance of the first passage or a physical phrase like "I blew my nose", in the end gives a human relief. They are the solid residue of a detailed observation of society. Gogol has selected the bold outline and essentials from a full notebook. He is writing about a town, a body of people. He is laughing at the Russian situation of the time. The book has significance beyond its laughter and yet laughter and pity engulf that significance too. There are two very moving passages—and Gogol is always surprising the reader by his changes of mood as well as by the changes of the antics of his characters—one when Chichikov takes home the list of "dead peasants" and studies first the manner in which each landowner has written his list, this one casually, another with precision and remarks, and then meditates, Hamlet-like, on the fates and habits of the dead serfs. This passage deepens the joke until it touches the seriousness of men's lives and directs our eyes from the laughter of the moment to the irony of eternity. The other passage is the apostrophe to Russia and her mission in the world. From Gogol onwards this nostalgia for spiritual greatness is one of the most moving things in Russian literature. We are moved by it because of the strangeness of meeting a nationalism rooted not in pride but in humility. This humility and this disinterestedness have given the Russian novel its supreme place in European literature.

Dead Souls belongs to that group of novels which most novelists dream of writing. I mean the picaresque or novel of travel, in which the episodic adventures of a single character open up the world. Given the brilliant idea the task, it seems, should be easy. Yet has there been such a novel of any quality since, say, *David Copperfield*? I can think of none. It seems that the appearance of the picaresque literature depends on the existence of disorder in society. In *Pickwick*, we remember, "boilers were busting and the minds of coachmen were unsettled"; in the Spain of Cervantes, the new gold wealth of the Spanish Empire had destroyed the value of money and had brought misery. In the Russia of *Dead Souls* tyranny was struggling to hold down the unrest of hope and vision which had followed the Napoleonic wars. What is necessary to this kind of novelist is a time of lethargy, cynicism and low comedy, a time when romantic idealism would be thwarted and when wry laughter at the roguery and fatuousness of people would be the only outlet. Our own society has been too prosperous for this kind of book, for a prosperous society is without humour or pity. Is that an explanation of the decline in the picaresque novel? Or is it simply that the kind has been done too often and is now exhausted?

A HERO OF OUR OWN TIME

In the February of 1848 Turgenev left Brussels for Paris where he joined Bakunin. They had come to see a revolution. Five months later, namely in the sultry afternoon of the 26th of July, Turgenev was out in the streets watching the revolution collapse. He watched, he noted, he deplored. When it was over he did not, for all his love of Liberty, share that sense of personal tragedy which overcame the Herzen circle. Herzen wished now that he had taken a rifle which a workman had offered him and had died upon the barricades. "I would then", he said, "have taken with me to the grave one or two beliefs." But Turgenev, who believed in "the homeopathy of science and education", shrugged his shoulders. "What is history, then? Providence, chance, irony or fatality?" he asked Pauline Viardot. He paid Bakunin his allowance, he made jokes to break the gloom of the Herzen household. The dogmas and violence of active politicians had little attraction for Turgenev though he liked to think that his *Sportsman's Sketches* had popularised the idea of freeing the serfs in Russian society.

But it was impossible in that decade for a Russian writer to escape from politics, and seven years later, when his lethargic nature stirred and he sat down to write his first political novel, Turgenev turned again to those sultry days in Paris. Always in doubt about his characters, subject to all the waverings of sensibility, running round to his friends for advice because he had no confidence in his own judgment, Turgenev managed, at last, and like a naturalist, to pin his hero to the paper. In his memory Turgenev saw once more the Faubourg St. Antoine,

the barricades and the broken revolutionaries dribbling away
from them in furtive groups. As a line battalion came up
and the last workmen ran for their lives, he imagined a solitary
figure rising up on the barricade. He was "a tall man in an
old overcoat, with a red sash and a straw hat on his grey, dishevelled hair. In one hand he held a red flag, in the other a
blunt curved sabre, and as he scrambled up he shouted something in a shrill, strained voice, waving his flag and sabre. A
Viennese shooter took aim at him—fired." The tall man
fell with a bullet in his heart.

" 'Tiens!' " said one of the escaping revolutionaries to
another, " ' on vient de tuer le polonais.' " So, with an in-
eptitude for his epitaph, died the Russian Dimitri Rudin. He
had died, cutting a figure on a foreign barricade for a cause
not his own, futile to the end.

I first read *Rudin* during the Spanish Civil War. It was a
good moment. For years we had been talking about the
problem of the intellectual for whom society has no use—
that is to say we had been talking about all the English intellectuals who had grown up since 1914—for years we had
argued the reasons for this isolation, its effects upon their
minds and had speculated upon their future. The figure
of Rudin seemed to crystallise the case. And when one more
angry friend from Bloomsbury packed up his books and his
chequered love affairs and went out to be killed in the Spanish
war, we could picture the scene at once and swear we heard
some Spanish soldier revise Rudin's insulting epitaph once
more, with a "God, they've killed the German". The English
have always been Germans in Spain.

It was thought at first that Bakunin had been Turgenev's
model for Rudin, and Turgenev encouraged the belief; but
Herzen observed that there was a good deal of Turgenev
himself in this minor Hamlet. In fact, Rudin was drawn
from several models. He was Bakunin on the barricades and

luckier than his original in dying there; he was any gifted young Russian whom political tyranny at home had reduced to futility: and he was Turgenev in love. Perhaps Turgenev was getting the Bakunin family out of his system and all the philosophy of his German period too, for there are unflattering resemblances between Turgenev's affair with Bakunin's sister and Rudin's cold-hearted experiments with the heart of Natalya. There are really two Rudins in the book and the critic must decide for himself whether he is dealing with two irreconcilable beings, the idealist and the cad, or whether Turgenev is showing an eye for the variety and inconsistency of human nature. One thing is plain, as it always is when social types are analysed in fiction, that Turgenev had a theory. We must not ask why Rudin appeared in Russia, one of the characters says, one must merely examine him; but Turgenev leaves one in little doubt about the social and political reasons for his existence.

It is often assumed that tyranny can conquer everything except the intelligence, but the briefest glance at history shows that this residue of optimism is without foundation. The aim and effect of tyranny is to break up the normal social relations between people and to ensure that the only permitted social relationship shall be with the tyrant. Our duty is not to our neighbour, but to the leader, the tyrant, the ruling oligarchy, and this duty isolates us from each other whether we think of ourselves as individuals or as groups. Once isolated like this the mind degenerates, faculties stray and purpose falls to pieces. Upon the intelligence the effect is immediate, for the intellectual man, who seems to be so independent of the mass of mankind because of his brains, in fact needs the moral background of normal social relations more strongly than anyone else. Without them he is like a sculptor who, deprived of stone, is obliged to carve in the air. We see this plainly enough in the lives of the exiles from German and Italian Fascism; we shall see it again if we consider the isolation of the English intellectuals in the Big Business tyranny which impoverished the material, spiritual and intellectual life of England in the years leading up to the present war. There was a choice between two evils: the futility of exile, the futility of a life at home which had been carefully unco-ordinated. In the Russia of the 'forties despotism had driven the active into exile; those who would not or could not leave were obliged to preserve their ideas in a vacuum or to while away their time on mere personal speculation which grew more and more esoteric.

When Rudin arrives at Darya Mihailovna's country house, he is a man of 35. He is shy at first, sizing up his company. Soon he is drawn into argument with one of those strutting, professional sceptics who hide a general lack of information under the disguise of being plain, downright fellows who say, 'To hell with principles, give me the facts'. Rudin-Turgenev has not been a philosopher for nothing; he wipes the floor with this eccentric. Rudin's polish, his heart and his eloquence arouse a generous response in the company and in the reader. We are delighted with him. But he stays on with Darya Mihailovna, and as he stays we get to know him better. A longer acquaintance does not confirm the first favourable impression. Those glorious words of Rudin's, for example, were not his own; that passionate idealism has no recognisable earthly objective. He can settle to nothing. The enthusiasm which would be admirable in a man of 20 is suspect in a man of 35 who ought to have built up some stability. Bassistoff, the young tutor, cries out that Rudin is a natural genius. "Genius very likely he has," replies Lezhnyov, "but as for being natural—that's just his misfortune, that there's nothing natural in him. . . ." He is a mere oracle of the boudoir and a fake.

In the next phase Turgenev strikes nearer home: Rudin is far too expert in the egoism of romantic love. He knows the whole keyboard from the evocation of "pure souls" to the effectiveness of a melancholy hint at incurable fate:

"Look," began Rudin with a gesture towards the window, "do you see that apple tree?   It is broken by the weight and abundance of its own fruit.   True emblem of genius."

Rudin is as cold as ice and he will do nothing unless his vanity is aroused; then he behaves like a pompous and meddlesome idiot and discovers he has done so half an hour too late.   For he is introspective.   Philosophy—we have exchanged it for psycho-analysis—has got into his blood and he is interested only in the doomed course of his own development.   And this coldness of Rudin which leads him skilfully to awaken the feeling of inexperienced women and particularly those very young ones whose feeling is maternal, and then to take fright before their dullness, is of long-standing.   He had been too much adored by his mother.

The Rudin of our generation would have had more to say about this mother.   The Russian Rudin says little or nothing, and Turgenev tells only that the cold youth dropped her, as he dropped all his friends.   Did he hate her?   Turgenev does not say.   That field, so fruitful to our contemporaries, is neglected.   We know simply that Rudin's lack of means and career is an excellent excuse for running away from marriage, and we can only guess at a deeper dread of reproducing the pattern that made him.   Rudin is homeless politically and emotionally, and if he *had* had a career and a place in society, he would have had to retreat into more complex justifications—as nowadays the Rudin in us does.

But if he tortures others Rudin tortures himself, too.   After the affair with Natalya, there is an interlude of desperate farce.   Philosophy (to which he has retired) tells him he should allow himself to fall really in love and so wipe out his guilt, and in Germany he tries out a passion to order with a French dressmaker. Alas, the old Adam remains. Seated in a boat Rudin gazes at the lady, pats her gently on the head—and tells her he feels like a father to her. He had been a brother to Natalya.

And now Rudin is nothing but a cad, Turgenev makes his severest critic, the mature and decent Lezhnyov, take everything back. This is the most exciting point in the novel. This new Rudin is not as vivid as the old one, he has the weakness—perhaps it is due to Turgenev's old-fashioned, hearsay technique as a story teller—of being a point of view and an afterthought. But a warmth *is* put into the old outline and the figure is at last taken out of the psychologist's bottle and related to his environment:

> He has enthusiasm; and believe me, who am a phlegmatic person enough, that is the most precious quality of our times. We have all become insufferably reasonable, indifferent and slothful; we are asleep and cold, and thanks to anyone who will wake us up and warm us. . . . He is not an actor, as I called him, nor a cheat, nor a scoundrel; he lives at other people's expense, not like a swindler, but like a child. . . .

(Herzen had said almost these very words of Bakunin).

> Who has the right to say that he has not been of use? That his words have not scattered good seeds in young hearts, to whom nature has denied, as she has to him, power for action and the faculty of carrying out their ideas?

This is all very nice, and Bassistoff, for the younger generation, cries out, "Bravo!" But is it nature that has denied Rudin the power for action? We come nearer truth (and nearer to-day) as Lezhnyov proceeds:

> Rudin's misfortune is that he does not understand Russia, and that, certainly, is a great misfortune. Russia can do without every one of us, but not one of us can do without her. Woe to him who thinks he can, and woe two-fold

to him who actually does do without her!   Cosmopolitanism
is all twaddle, the cosmopolitan is a nonentity; without
nationality is no art, nor truth, nor life, nor anything. . . .
It would take us too far if we tried to trace Rudin's origin
among us.

It was not Rudin's fault that 1848 was not 1917.   It was
to his credit that he half-killed himself and his wretched companion when they went "up to the river in the province of
K.", with the hare-brained scheme of making it navigable,
several generations before the Five Year Plan gave intelligent
men something to do.   Rudin not only sowed the seed, but
with some courage he accepted the knowledge of foredoomed
failure, the destiny and the ridicule that watches over the
sower who cannot hope to reap.   Mean in his egoism, he was
not mean in his imagination.

Turgenev considered the figure of Rudin from an uneasy
seat on the liberal fence.   By nature timid and hesitant, he
resisted the notion of dramatic choice.   And we must remember, too, that he wrote of Rudin when there was no flush of
belief in Europe.   He was writing in 1855, seven years after
the "Viennese shooter" had taken aim, in the lethargy of
disillusion.   When Herzen's conversion to communism was
complete Turgenev broke with him.

FAITS DIVERS

I HAVE been reading Dostoevski again: *The Possessed*. You know the sensation. You are sitting by the fire reflecting that one of the things which reconciles you to life, even at its most tragic, is the low clear daily monotone of its voice. Suddenly comes a knock at the door, there are cries. A man has been murdered at a house down the street. Dostoevski again. Dostoevski, "the great sinner", the great literary murderer. You put on your thickest coat and go out. What a fog! What a melodramatic fog. You can see nothing. Such is the impression as one turns to those tortured novels again. But there's obviously a crowd somewhere down the road, you can hear voices, people go rushing by. Who is it this time? Shatov, you hear, the student, the ex-radical, the believer in the Russian Christ. Good heavens! There was no one more serious, more honest, more likeable than Shatov; rather difficult in argument because he had never got over a sort of angry awkwardness about his class. He was tongue-tied and shy one moment, violently angry the next. His anger soon passed, however, and then he smiled repentantly. There was absolutely no malice in Shatov. You hurry down the street, still seeing nothing. Shapes move about. They may be human. You call to them and they gesticulate but you can't hear what they're saying. Presently you make a disconcerting discovery, that you are in something like one of Kafka's nightmares; you are walking and yet making no progress. You begin to wonder which street you're in. People bump into you and don't answer questions. No one in Dostoevski ever answers questions. You just detect a scowling face which shouts at you. This one (he says he's an engineer), shouts that he is going to commit suicide. It is necessary to commit suicide to show that he has overcome fear of pain and the beyond. When he has done this he will be God, the Man-God, the superman. He vanishes. A girl shape stands dumbly in front of you; she desires, you gather, to suffer. Which way to the murder? you ask. No answer. Terrible complications. The air full of the sounds of people talking. A drunken Captain is beating his daughter and quoting poetry. You turn a corner and there is a young nobleman, handsome, cultivated, thoughtful, and what is he doing? He's biting the Governor's ear. And still, as in one of those anxiety dreams, your feet stick to the pavement, you make enormous, concentrated efforts of will, and you move about an inch instead of a yard. The fog chokes. "Russia, the god-fearing nation," someone shouts. "Let us start an illegal printing press," a girl says. "Destroy everything", come other voices, "and then a new man will be born, a new society, harmonious, communistic, brotherly." Or "Russia's mission is to save the world". And another voice, "Russia must save Germany first from the catastrophe which is coming inevitably in the West." And what is the catastrophe? "Socialism! Socialism is the despotism of materialism, the ally of the Roman Catholic Church in the destruction of the soul." You struggle towards that voice only to be pulled in the opposite direction by another. "Christianity, communism, through the People and the purification of the heart." At this moment you very nearly fall over a man who is on his knees before a woman, abased, weak and weeping; she is pulling his hair out. "Love-hate," they are murmuring. "Who", you ask, "are all these people, all these voices?" A moan comes from the man: "Relations," he says, "everyone has brought his relations."

And then, the tension of the nightmare slackens, the fog clears and along come a middle-aged couple and you laugh

for the first time. The humour in Dostoevski always clears
the fog. They are quarrelling, of course. The man is talking
all the time. "Chère amie," he says, as she gives him a violent
push to make him shut up. Scholarly, noble-looking, vague
and slopping a glass of champagne, Stepan Trofimovitch is
straying and tottering along, pouring out epigrams, tag ends
of French and cultural chit-chat. He will stop to make a
speech about his dangerous political past and is alarmed the
moment afterwards lest a spy has heard him or, worse still,
in case someone lets on that he has no political past whatever
and certainly no political future. And behind him comes
Varvara Petrovna, twenty years his protector and his "amie"
but only in the sense that he used to smoke a cigar under the
lilac tree with her in the evenings. A female rolling-pin, a
torment and manager, dusting him, cleaning him up, mocking his
feebleness, rating him about his gambling debts, but paying them,
awed by his brains. For the last twenty years he has talked of
beginning his great book. But there are the club, his cards, the
perpetual apprehension of what Varvara Petrovna will do next.
He must leave her; he can't leave her. Varvara Petrovna is
another Madame de Staël whacking into her pet, Benjamin
Constant. She pushes her tame intellectual and toy liberal along.

Man was born free, but not necessarily born with will or
cash. What does man achieve? Nothing, except habits. On
top of everything, Stepan has been married so many times. It
is years since he has seen his son. How terrible the separation
of father and son—and yet, just as well, for Stepan Trofimovitch
has never been quite straight about money. So he goes on,
speaking French, weeping, evading, making noble gestures,
cheating, scenting his handkerchief, making "final stands" about
the intrigues of Varvara Petrovna—though not in her presence
—while she, the masterful *intrigante*, frankly tells him he's a
fool and that she's going to send a servant round to clean up,
and then marry him off.

The nightmare, of course, again intercepts that comic intrigue. The fog comes down once more. But you have been distracted from the suicides, ear-biters, daughter-beaters and ideological murderers. As you grope once more it is the figure of Stepan Trofimovitch you seek, the bold voice of Varvara Petrovna you long to hear. He is in love and hates her, but with *them* the love-hate is nostalgia and comedy. And then the nightmare affects Stepan Trofimovitch, too. He *does*, to his own astonishment, make a "last stand". He walks out of the house. He is like that. He will take to the road. They said he had not the will to do anything for an idea! That his idealism was a fraud! He goes forth as exalted as Don Quixote (though far more rattled) follows a cow which is following some peasants, flabbergasts them by talking French, picks up with a Bible-seller, and rambles away, tragically, comically, but far from ignobly, to his death. Vanity is a friend to him to the end; it enables him to humbug on the very brink of eternity (this time about the Sacrament) and prevents him from realising he is dying. It is he who explains the whole nightmare to you, all that fog, talk, intrigue, violence; who all these people are. They are "The Possessed", "the devils", and with the detachment of a well-stocked intellect he announces half-nobly, half-cynically, that "he and everyone else in Russian politics are the Gadarene swine of Russia which must all be cleared out and driven to the sea, so that the wonderful new future may be born".

The Possessed is a novel which contains one of the great comic characters of all literature; and the first 150 pages contain the best writing in Dostoevski's surprising comic vein. Lytton Strachey was the first to point out the individuality and importance of Dostoevski's humour. It steadies those toppling and seemingly intoxicated monuments. Critics usually refer to this gift as satirical, but as Lytton Strachey said, the humour is not cruel. If it begins cruelly it grows, deepens

and broadens into the humour of loving-kindness. But there
are other reasons for reading *The Possessed*. It is a political
novel which—though many of its premises are derived from
inaccurate information—deals prophetically with some of the
political issues of our time. Tolstoy, not very sensitive in his
old age, once said to Gorky that Dostoevski ought to have
been a Buddhist; and Gorky said of Dostoevski that "you could
tell a petit-bourgeois as surely as you could tell a goat". These
are amusing examples of a criticism which seems to be passing
out of fashion now that the fanatical Freudians and the narrower
kind of Marxist have discovered that they were not really
interested in literature. The only proper general political
criticism of Dostoevski is, as a recent American critic, Mr.
Ernest Simmons, has said, that he expresses the confusion in
Russian middle-class thought at the time, its ideals, its apprehension, its practice. We see the psychological discoveries
of Dostoevski in better perspective when we remember that
Constant and many others had written more precisely about
the ambivalence of human character. We cool down when
we reflect that the Self-Willed Man, the meek and the famous
"doubles of Dostoevski, are the fruits of the romantic movement which came to Russia late.

From the letters, diaries and notes of Dostoevski which have
been made available in Russia since the revolution, the curious
reader may discover that the fog he had been groping through
is nothing to the personal fog in which Dostoevski worked.
(I recommend anyone interested in the intimate processes of
literary creation to read Ernest Simmon's *Dostoevski: The
Making of a Novelist*[1]). The main character types are repeated
with growing emphasis from novel to novel, but they emerge
from a nightmare of rough drafts and notes. Dostoevski
worked in the greatest uncertainty and indecision. He was
one of those writers who, having for a long time no clear and

[1] Oxford University Press.

fixed idea of his intention, was obliged to lash himself into action by pious ejaculations. He worked, so to speak, on a stage, before an audience, delightfully unaware that there was something comic in his vociferations.

"I am planning" (when was he not "planning"?) "a huge novel" (they were always going to be "huge" and transcendental) "to be called *Atheism*—for God's sake between ourselves."

The touch of persecution mania is part of the show. Then: "the hero falls to the very depths of self-abasement and in the end he returns to find both Christ and the Russian soul. For God's sake do not tell anyone." Tortured as the reader of the novels may be, lost in the wilderness of a dialogue which has eliminated none of the drooling and rambling of humanity's eternal tongue-wagging, worried by the involutions of the plot and the fact that no character seems to be able to appear without half his family and without at least one family skeleton, he is nevertheless far more certain than Dostoevski himself was as he struggled at his desk. He chops and changes his characters and events. He has constantly to write down the theme of his novel again in order to remind himself of what he is doing; and the theme is always drifting off its course. The change has been noted in *Crime and Punishment*: Raskolnikoff was intended to suicide. Ivan was thought of as the murderer of Karamozov. If Dostoevski's life was a search for God, his novels are a search for a method. The higher synthesis which he laboured after and retreated from in religion, only to labour after it again, plagued him too in the art of writing. The thing that strikes one in Dostoevski's novels is how, both in their ideas and their method of presentation, they convey the struggle, the search for something to be born, the longing to assume a shape. But perhaps it is not a longing for form. Perhaps the profound longing of Dostoevski is to decide nothing for himself, but to be dominated. It is significant that a formal Westernised writer like Turgenev is hated, and that when Dostoevski looks beyond Russia, his eye stops at Germany. That domineering race has attractive wastes of primitive myth behind the façade of its culture; and when the great catastrophe comes Russia, he says, will save Germany from the West and Germany and Russia will save the world. It is curious that the Nazis did not make use of Dostoevski's mysticism, though it goes really far beyond nationalism into mysticism. The race myth is there:

> "If a great people [Shatov cries in *The Possessed*] does not believe that the truth is to be found in it alone (in itself alone and exclusively in itself), if it does not believe that it alone is fit and destined to raise up and save all by its truth, it at once ceases to be a great nation, and at once turns into ethnographical material and not into a great people. A truly great people can never reconcile itself with a secondary rôle in humanity or even with the first, but without fail must exclusively play the first rôle. A nation which loses this belief ceases to be a nation.

The Russians are, in fact—God-bearing!

It is useless to try and disentangle the confusions from the subtleties of Dostoevski's thought. The great prophets are always playing for both sides. And then Dostoevski is a Victorian journalist. There is always a less exalted strain of compromise running through Dostoevski's life, a sort of left-handed self-interest such as makes the comedy of Stepan Trofimovitch's character. There is frequently something disconcertingly practical if not disingenuous about the mystics. Ideologically, Dostoevski is often in a panic. Yet, there are two perennial kinds of revolutionary thought; there is the political revolutionary who arises to change man by changing society, the religious who arises to change society by changing man. Dostoevski is brought nearer to us also because the catastrophe has come, the problem of suffering has become real; and if we cannot believe in the absolute value of suffering, any

78

more than Dostoevski entirely did, it is arresting when we cry out egotistically against injustice to be reminded, as Zosima reminded Ivan Karamazov, of guilt.

Dostoevski was a spiritual sensationalist, a man of God somewhat stained with the printing ink of the late night final. He lives at first in the upper air as he plans his novels, and gradually comes down to earth, still undetermined until he is pulled up—by what? "Ordinary" life? No, a newspaper cutting. What a passion he has for the newspapers! What significance things had once they were in headlines! The report of the Nechaev affair clinches *The Possessed*, a *cause célèbre* sets the idea of *The Idiot* in motion. These court cases pinned down his restless mind. Early in *The Possessed* Liza asks Shatov to help her compile an annual collection of newspaper cuttings of all the court cases, trials, speeches, incidents and so on, the child-beatings, thefts, accidents, will-suits, etc., which would serve to give a real picture of the Russian situation year by year. Dostoevski must often have longed for a book like that on his desk. For ordinary people were lost in an anonymity which thwarted the romantic temperament. In the *faits divers* they were transformed; give him the evidence and the process of mystification could begin. The *faits divers* could become the *faits universels*.

THE CLOWN

For the civilised reader the psychological novel has been a most fascinating and flattering mirror, and egoism the delightful subject *par excellence*. But from Constant to Joyce and Proust the analysis of motive or of sensation has suffered from scientific priggishness and preciosity. Humour, in the sense of forgiveness, has not been the dominant trait. There is excellent humorous writing in Proust and Joyce, but the sustained note of those writers does not come from the dry, skipping, fiddle-strings of the comedians and buffoons. On the contrary, pitiless diagnosis is the note of Proust; and Joyce is driven on, not by laughter, but by a dishevelled hatred of the root of life. Disappointment and frustration seem to be inherent in the psychological approach, no doubt, because the assumption that we stand alone is fallacious. And in the novelists who have isolated themselves or their subjects, we cannot but observe that the analysis of character or sensation tends to degenerate into the desiccation of character; the surgery upon motives turns into a medical search for the diseased and monstrous ones.

To those who are in danger of reacting too violently against the great botanists of our hidden flora, I recommend the cure offered by the works of Italo Svevo. Here is laughter at last. Here Hamlet raises a smile, Œdipus is teased away from his fate like some figure of light opera, the *malade imaginaire* of the fag-end of the Romantic movement is made to get out of bed and run about in his pyjamas. The absurdities of life rescue us from the illusions of the intellect, from the grim stepmotherdom of our egoism and our brains. I do not mean that Svevo is a mere joker. He is far from that. He is no less sensitive or subtle in the elucidation of our feelings than the great botanists. The advantage of his laughter is that it makes his science humane and prevents his intelligence from dragging up our moral roots. And this is a point of huge importance to the development of the psychological novel. Over and over again we feel in such novels that the novelist is too knowingly superior to his people, his intelligence is too penetrating for the muddle of human nature. We suspect the sin of pride. That sin is entirely absent from the work of Svevo. He is the first of the psychological novelists to be beatified by a spirit of humility which recalls the battered but serene humility of *Don Quixote*, the humility of the comic tradition.

Very little is known in England about the life of Italo Svevo. Such information as we have comes from the introductions to his novels which were translated in the late 'twenties, and from the brother of James Joyce, who knew him well in Trieste. Joyce is said to have put something of Svevo into the portrait of Leopold Blum. Svevo's real name was Ettore Schmitz; he was born in 1861 and died in 1928. He lived most of his life in Trieste and was half-Italian, half-Austrian by origin. At the age of 32 he published his first novel, *Una Vita*, which was well received; five years later another novel, entitled *Senilità*, which was totally ignored. The fact that Svevo wrote in an Italian speckled by the impurities of the Trentino dialect was against him. He gave up literature for a business career in which he was very successful. Not until he was in his sixties did he write *La Coscienza di Zeno* (In English, *The Confessions of Zeno*), his most remarkable work, which he is said to have dashed off in a fortnight. The writing of this book and the fame it brought to Svevo owe something to the encouragement of Joyce, who, as a teacher of English in Trieste, had by chance been engaged by the business man to teach him our language. In his life the epicurean Svevo seems to have been robust, genial, solid, successful and urbane, the complete antithesis of the stoic Zeno, the brilliant, erratic hypochondriac, who is palmed off with marvellous skill as a self-portrait in *The Confessions*. Zeno was the hidden artist, an agile piece of mystification by an expert in loquacity. One can see a clue to the link between the solid Schmitz and the restless, forever enquiring and ever-deluded egoism of Zeno in the fact of Svevo's divided birth. He was one of the frontier people of Europe, of divided temperament, and was therefore perfectly fitted for the analytical passion in which one part of our nature sits on the fence and observes the other.

Senilità is itself not a very original book. It is the usual *étude de mœurs* on the favourite Latin theme of the *p'tite maîtresse*, the working-class girl who can be kept cheaply. The interest of the story lies in the humility of Svevo before his characters, in a studied naivety which foreshadows the manner of Kafka in the use of the method of unconscious revelation, i.e. of letting the psyche expose itself, and, finally, in Svevo's gift of writing epitaphs upon human feeling: "The thought of death is like an attribute of the body, a physical malady. Our will can neither summon it nor drive it away." The underlying subject of *Senilità* is illness—that is to say, the senility or second childishness of the illusions we live by, and this hidden subject gives the commonplace story its peculiar double plot.

But when *Zeno* was written, thirty years later, it was totally original and mature, and like *Adolphe*, contained the essence of a lifetime. Throwing chronology away, Svevo writes an autobiographical novel divided into subjects. The book is split up into reminiscent essays on his father, his marriage, his mistress and his business partnership, and, naturally, many of the episodes are concurrent. This unconventional method has the attractive carelessness of conversation. Moreover, the story is held together by an amusing framework. Zeno writes in order to debunk his psycho-analyst. According to his analyst, all Zeno's troubles—his troublesome love of his wife's sister, his hypochondria, his will-lessness, his nervous crises, his mad, restless brainwaves, heroic moral illusions, and his suspicions—are all due to the Œdipus complex. Zeno sets out to show life slipping like an eel through the stiff hands of this theory. At the end of the book he gives up psychoanalysis because, by chance, he runs across a doctor who tells him that his real disease is diabetes. Zeno is delighted. A régime at last, a new theory, a new order, the solution of all his problems! His wife remarks:

"My poor dear Zeno, you have talked so much during your life about illnesses that sooner or later you were bound to get one." And she overwhelmed me with tenderness.

However, neither Freud nor diabetes saves Zeno in the end. Obliged by the death and debts of his partner to attend seriously to his business, Zeno is saved by work. The intellectual is a natural gambler. He slaves (successfully) on the Bourse.

On its formal side Svevo's originality springs from high spirits, from sheer wit and brain, such as are found in a comedy of Beaumarchais or Sheridan. When we turn to his matter, we see that Svevo belongs to that rare number of novelists—almost non-existent in modern literature—who like their characters and side with them instead of destroying them piecemeal. And in Zeno, Svevo is engaged in liking the kind of character who is most vulnerable to disapproval. For Zeno is the egoist of all the egoists. How Meredith would have detached the pomposity and complacency from that ubiquitous first person singular! Zeno is in love with explanation. He is perpetually button-holing and explaining. He would have been the supreme café bore of Trieste. Now he is fantasticating about his struggles to give up smoking; now he is being unguardedly complacent about his wife, his ideals as a seducer, his mental superiority to his more experienced business partner, and so on. But Zeno has one saving virtue; he never believes

his own self-justifications. Zeno is just as happy when he
is grotesquely wrong as when he is accidentally right. He is
always on the damaging and humbling search for truth. Under
the café gabble of Zeno's enthusiastic tongue there lies a personal humility and tenderness, an exquisite ear for the true
tune of human living, an unshockable wonder at each transient
mystery of our feelings. Zeno *appears* to be a weak and
vacillating mad-hatter—and obtuse critics have attacked the
figure of Zeno as an example of the neurotic bourgeois who
suffers from a kind of intellectual diarrhœa—but, in fact, the
abiding impression he leaves is one of moral gravity.

The exaggerations which spring from the tradition of Italian
farce are the making of *The Confessions of Zeno*. The absurd
is trained upon the serious in order to awaken our emotions
from the conventional turgidity into which they habitually
settle. Two episodes illustrate the macabre and disturbing
effect of Svevo's use of bizarre incident. The first occurs in
the very moving and faithful account of the death of Zeno's
father. As usual, Zeno is overwrought, his emotions have
got beyond him. In his love for the dying father with whom
he has nothing in common, Zeno is quarrelling with everyone
at the sick-bed. With the scorn of youth, he has always
regarded his father as a weak man; but at the moment of
dying the old man rises in his bed as if he is going at last to
reveal the mystery of life and death to his son and to embrace
him; instead, the old man inadvertently hits him a blow on the
cheek and dies. It is unexpected, it is ridiculous, it is terrifying.
Literature abounds in deathbed scenes. To this one Svevo
has given a particularity which is memorable, not only because
it is eccentric, but because its effect on Zeno's character is
shown with real perspicacity. From that moment Zeno's
haunting illusion of weakness is dated. It is as illusory, of
course, as his earlier illusion of being stronger than his father.

The second episode is more truly farcical, and not macabre

at all. Svevo is again observing how life does not play up to conventional emotion, nor indeed to any theory at all. Guido, Zeno's partner and brother-in-law, has died. Zeno has always disapproved of him because Guido was a chronic womaniser, but chiefly because Guido had married the sister whom Zeno had once wished to marry. Zeno could never in consequence be sure of the honesty of his disapproval, as indeed he could never be sure of anything in his life. But, obviously, now Guido was dead, the tangle had been cut. Moreover, to show that he was really devoted to Guido, Zeno slaves day after day at the office until the very hour of the funeral, in order to clear up the shady financial mess in which Guido had left his affairs and so preserve Guido's good name. Give Zeno an illusion to preserve and he works for it with the fever of a lover. And then, when he is exhausted, Zeno suddenly remembers the funeral. He dashes out, hires a cab and begins a frantic search of the city for the funeral procession. His sister-in-law, whom he has always loved, will never forgive him if he fails to turn up at the funeral. At last the procession is found. The cab joins it and Zeno and his clerk sit back and relax to talk about the Bourse. Thank heaven. They are doing the conventional thing, for Zeno, like so many of the aberrated, has a longing for the conventional. And then they discover they are in the Greek cemetery. Guido was a Catholic. Obviously, they have followed the wrong funeral.

Four books by Svevo are available in English and are admirably translated by Beryl de Zoete. They include two collections of short stories which suffer from being brief restatements of the longer books. They are *The Hoax* and *The Nice Old Man and the Pretty Girl*. I find the Svevo of the short stories too playfully charming and serene, though *The Hoax* does define his quality:

> . . . a humble life, endowed with a kind of strength that comes from absolute surrender. . . .

Svevo sees our lives hanging in suspense from minute to minute; we appear, as we must do to the psychologist, to be in continual process of disintegration. And yet, surveying the scene again in longer stretches of time, there is, under the breathless chasing of illusions, a process of reintegration, too. The fool becomes the strong man, the younger son marries the ugly sister, who turns out to be the beautiful princess. And the business man of Trieste, ignored by literary society, is avenged by the brilliant, serious and hypochondriacal clown.

THE NOBODIES

IF my guess is right, this year or next is the centenary of
Mr. Pooter and maybe of Mr. Padge, Mr. Gowing and
Mr. Cummings as well. The patriotic historians of Holloway
should be at work, scheming for a plaque to be placed over
the doorway of The Laurels (No. 12), Brickfield Terrace.
There Mr. Pooter with his "dear wife" Carrie and his atrocious
son, Lupin, finally settled, and, in '91, when Mr. Pooter's
"grand old master" presented the freehold of the place to his
faithful clerk, he must have been 50. That, as the saying
is, takes one back; indeed, it is so far back for some of us that
we cross the frontier of comedy and enter into the wilderness
where family ends and history begins. The joke dims and
dims until it ceases to be a joke and becomes a fact.

The fact, neutral, normal, pathetic, is the essence of the
humour of *The Diary of a Nobody*. Gentility was the illusion;
the grim fact was that Mr. Pooter was not very well off, that
he tripped on doorscrapers, that he ate Wednesday's blancmange
on Thursday and Friday in holy matrimonial privacy and was
caught doing the same on Saturday by the brutal Gowing who
shouted out *while the servant was in the room*, "Hulloh! The
remains of Wednesday." Facts were the fly in Mr. Pooter's
ointment, the Gowing in the laurel bush. Off pops his made-
up tie at the ball, out "in Society" he is horrified to meet his
ironmonger, the laundry returns his coloured handkerchief
without the colour, and his wife violates the sanctity of marriage
by complaining, "in company", that every morning she has
to listen to his "blessed" dreams. For years he has laboured
and reached that summit where a man can at last open a bottle

of three-and-sixpenny champagne with an air both festive and refined, only to discover that this is not a summit but a foothill. Indeed he has to listen to Mr. Hardfur Huttle saying that it is insult and murder to give your guests even a six-shilling champagne. Mr. Pooter's life is one long humiliation at the hands of triviality and God gave him no gift of laughing at himself. Far from this, the only things he can laugh at are his own jokes—puns brought forth after long preparation which only "dear Carrie" sees and then not always—and though as sensitive in the trills of decorum as the Cid was on the point of honour, he is doomed to be pestered all his life by the enraging bites of petty indignity. A boob, a fool, a tedious and touchy old bore, Mr. Pooter has the innocence but not the stature of the comic martyrs; he is a study in the negative; he is a good man in the sense that the Devil evidently regards him as being too dull for temptation. The Evil One is content to put hard peas in the shoes of the pilgrim on the trim avenues of gentility and to leave him to it.

The foreigner who picked up *The Diary of a Nobody* would be bound to note that there must have been something especially dreary about English lower middle-class life in the 'nineties. I hear echoes of elderly relatives saying "Poor So-and-so" was a "cure" or "a caution", that he or she was always saying and doing things which were "too real". Reality was the joke, its awful, dreary greyness. People who, like "dear Carrie", turned the leg of mutton over and covered it with parsley so that the unexpected visitor would not notice the joint had been cut, laughed at the little comedy when they read about it or saw it on the stage. There is a pathos in a joke so small, a Cockney whine, a cringing suggestion of the prison house. Yet it would be a mistake to regard the humour of the Grossmiths as a sedative to its audience, an aid to complacency or resignation. Looking down upon snobbery, we see the comedy of snobbery; looking up to it, we see what a dynamic romantic force it has been in English middle-class life, how it is natural to an expanding society. The words "too real" are not a pathetic acceptance of life's little domestic ironies only; they are an idealistic protest against reality, a call to push on with the illusion, to afford a really uncut shoulder of mutton in the house next time. The moral impulse in the English character takes peculiar and generally vulgar forms. Like the go-getting Japanese, we dare not lose face, and the cultivation of dignity, ambivalence and vulgarity to this end is automatic with us.

As "too-realists" the Grossmiths were salutary historians. They recorded the paralysis of middle-class living, the horror when the preoccupation with etiquette, with good manners and bad manners, was upset by someone like Mr. Padge who had no manners at all, not even bad ones. Mr. Padge, that low man who seemed all moustache, who took the best chair and would not budge from it all the evening, who stared at everybody, smoked a dirty pipe and whose only words were "That's right" and who had a coarse, vacuous laugh, is a great character:

> I was so annoyed at the conduct of Padge, I said: "I suppose you would have laughed if he had poked Mr. Gowing's eye out?" to which Padge replied "That's right", and laughed more than ever.

And yet the Grossmiths are just; they are never savage, never unkind; they trip Mr. Pooter but they help him up afterwards; they leave to insipidity its native pathos. The fact that Mr. Pooter himself is recording his daily hopes and disasters in all their shattering mildness, keeps us on his side. One cannot kick a man when he is down; one cannot ridicule a man who is already making an ass of himself in his diary. One feels protective towards the Mr. Pooter who is so childishly engaged in curling the whiskers and adjusting the coat-tails of the proprieties that, when life breaks through in the form of a slap-stick bread fight, a row with the butcher or "words" with his son, he is always helpless and hides his nakedness with indignation. And indignation, of course, makes it worse. English humour on its cheerfully vulgar course always ends in knock-about:

> They then commenced throwing hard pieces of crust, one piece catching me on the forehead, and making me blink. I said: "Steady, please; steady!" Frank jumped up and said: "Tum, tum, then the band played."
> I did not know what this meant, but they roared and continued the bread battle. Gowing suddenly seized all the parsley off the cold mutton and threw it in my face. I looked daggers at Gowing who replied: "I say, it's no good trying to look indignant, with your hair full of parsley." I rose from the table and insisted that a stop should be put to this foolery at once. Frank Mutlar shouted, "Time, gentlemen, please, time," and turned out the gas, leaving us in complete darkness.

Yes, one feels protective to Mr. Pooter; he is innocent. The truly comic character always is. From Don Quixote down to Pickwick, Pooter and Beachcomber's Mr. Thake.

The Diary of a Nobody was the sane answer to the sentimental realism of Gissing. The "too real" had reached a stage in Gissing which was altogether too real. There is an incredible story of Gissing's which describes how a young lady from Balham broke off her engagement and ruined her life because of the shame of discovering that a photograph of herself as a baby had appeared in the public Press to advertise a Baby Food. The need for laughter was obviously urgent. But each age provides its own antidote in the younger generation. In the *Diary* there is nothing so fascinating sociologically as the character of the awful son Lupin, that bouncing, insubordinate and loud young man who is always being sacked from his jobs only, against all desert, to get much better and also much shadier ones. Lupin is a symptom. The prim mid-Victorians have given birth to the effusively vulgar Edwardians, the exuberant business man is succeeding to the industrious clerk and "the grand old master"; just as the stucco and yellow brick of Brickfield Terrace is to be abandoned—shortly to become a slum—and will be superseded by the red brick, balconies and Tudor of the next ring of suburbia. The sulking, the shiftiness, the flashiness of Lupin are perfect. He is of his time and yet he has touches of the eternal.

Much of *The Diary of a Nobody* is dated in fact and in general atmosphere. The happy ending, so natural, is quite dated. At 50 the present-day Pooters do not get a rise of £100 a year; they get the sack. They are too old. As for "the grand old master", the Pooters of to-day never see their employers, hardly know who they are. Most of us would be glad to know our ironmongers. The humorous writing which was a kind of comic game of chess with the English class system survives in only the feeblest artificial comedy of the commercial stage, and the commercial stage is usually a generation behind the times. With the loss of class as a comic subject, kindness has gone because stability has gone. Our own humour is more cruel. It is speedier and prefers fantasy, as is shown by a glance at Beachcomber—the Grossmiths' successor. Why, then, does the *Diary* still amuse? Like an old fashion, of course; but also because it was the most economical, the least wordy, the most limpid and crystalline of its kind; because it anticipated the *sans commentaire* method which is characteristic of today. Its popularity with the older generation of whom Mr. Pooter was the ridiculous father, where to us he is an archaic and hardly known grandparent, springs from the general relief it brought to the mid-Victorian strain; it was a new humour of the lower middle-class which Wells and Bennett (a pair of Lupins in their time) were to carry further, and which was disapproved of by the refined. It is interesting to read of the disgust which this new voice of the lower middle-class aroused when it became heard at the beginning of the century. The objection of the aristocratic critic of the *Morning Post*, for example, to Jerome's *Three Men in a Boat*, was to the lowness of its people. The subtle *Diary* disarmed that critic by satirising the gentility he had taught them.

A VICTORIAN MISALLIANCE

THE epic of the free speech and little things—so that heroic critic, the late G. K. Chesterton, described Robert Browning's *The Ring and the Book*. Here was a giant whom the great rescuer of giants in distress found irresistible. Twice as long as the *Æneid*, twice as long as *Paradise Lost*, twice as long as the *Odyssey* and one-third as long as the *Iliad*, Browning's poem is obviously a great something, if only a great miscarriage. As epic, I think, despite Chesterton's brilliant special pleading, it is not, and precisely for the reasons which he gives for the view. Epics deal with great things, not little things; they describe not humanity free but humanity bound by the primitive chains of Fate, ruled by some absolute tribunal of value or dogma. No such fixed or majestic background stands behind the Renaissance police-court story on which Browning based *The Ring and the Book*; on the contrary, the very nature of the search for Truth, which is Browning's substitute, is that it is fluid, restless, uncertain, evolutionary. The stepping-stones by which we rise from our dead selves to higher things ascend into a mist and disappear from sight.

What Browning did produce was a great Victorian novel or, more accurately, the child of a misalliance between poetry and the novel. The Franceschini murder was essentially a novelist's subject; it was as much concerned with intrigues of property as it was with the aspirations and corruption of the soul. One's mind wanders to another nineteenth-century writer who had also found his subject in the *faits divers*. Just as Flaubert patiently wrote out the dossier of a similar scandal from Rouen and added to it the alloy of his own love-affair

with Louise Colet and made *Madame Bovary,* so Browning
put something of Elizabeth Barrett into his seventeenth-century
Pompilia, and from the memory of his unforgettable crisis of
conscience at the time of the elopement—an adventure in
which, he felt, he had been on the brink of murder—narrated
that flight with Caponsacchi, the priest, which was to lead to
Pompilia's death. Poetry abstracts drama from the dossier;
Browning reverses the process. Finding the drama concise
and abstract in the famous yellow book picked up on the second-
hand bookstall in Rome, he multiplied and analysed it into
the point of view of every possible spectator of the case. Not
only were the leading characters given their say, but he collected the common gossip of the streets and even parodied his
own subject in the two books which describe the esoteric high
jinks of the lawyers. The poem is clamorous with rival voices
of people; real people with characters, coats, hats, trades, names
and addresses. This impression was not lost on Henry James.
The great rival collector of Italian curiosities saw that *The
Ring and the Book* was a Henry James novel gone wrong—not
long enough among other things!

It is curious to note how these two Victorian connoisseurs
moved instinctively towards a tale of scandal and spiritual
corruption. The period's growing interest in crime, its love
of melodrama and its feeling for corruption have considerable
social interest. The preoccupation grows stronger as the great
bourgeois period becomes self-confident. Flaubert spent his
life collecting objects of disgust; Henry James had the shocked
expression of a bishop discovering something unspeakable in a
museum; Browning, the casuist, becomes in Chesterton's
excellent words "a kind of cosmic detective who walked into
the foulest of thieves' kitchens and accused men publicly of
virtue." (If one resents Browning's optimism today it is
because of this ingenious complacency; surely one should
accuse thieves of being thieves.) To be more particular, the

thieves' kitchens were a traditional interest of the Browning family. They had delicate consciences which were awkwardly allied to exuberant natures. Suburban Camberwell had been unable to contain the imaginations of the Bank of England clerk or of his precocious son. Sunday strollers, as they passed the Browning villa, could not have suspected that, inside, a child and his father were re-enacting the siege of Troy with chairs and tables, spouting epics and medieval romances to each other, re-arguing the battles of forgotten pedants, revelling in the dubious intrigue, the passion and the poisons of the Continent, and all the time keeping up to the minute on the crime story of the week. A man of the eighteenth century and a clerk, Browning's father easily kept this learned escapism cool. The heroic couplet, as practised by Pope, did a good deal to soothe his savage breast. But it was otherwise in the nineteenth-century son. Liberty was in the air, shape lost its symmetry, energy blew itself out into the sublime or the grotesque.

The Ring and the Book is one of those detective stories in which we are given the crime and the murderer at the beginning. We are given an event as we ourselves might read of it in the newspaper and the object is to discover what is true and what is false in everyone's story and in the crowd's conjecture. Browning's method complicates and recomplicates the suspense, shifts us from one foot to the other in growing agitation and excitement before the mystery.

Do we feel for Pompilia, still not dead, with twenty-five dagger-wounds in her? Very little. One is, of course, more moved than one is by the conventional corpse of a detective story; but not vastly more. The true incentive is to the brain, in watching this pile of evidence mount up and the next "point of view" undermine it. Now we are thrown into the common gossip of Rome and no one excels Browning in the rendering of rumour, scandal and the tunnellings of common insinuation:

At last the husband lifted an eyebrow—bent
On day-book and the study how to wring
Half the due vintage from the worn-out vines
At the villa, tease a quarter the old rent
From the farmstead, tenants swore would tumble soon—
Picked up his ear a-singing day and night
With "ruin, ruin"—and so surprised at last—
Why, what else but a titter?   Up he jumps
Back to mind come those scratchings at the grange,
Prints of the paw about the outhouse; rife
In his head at once again are word and wink,
Mum here and *budget* there, the smell o' the fox,
The musk of the gallant.   "Friends, there's
　　falseness here!"

The case for Pompilia and her priests never quite recovers from the effectiveness of Franceschini's defence. His story is a false one. He is as villainous as Iago; all the better he draws his own character: the down-at-heel noble, rich in tradition, empty in purse—"a brainful of belief, the noble's lot"—cynical no doubt, but look how he has been treated; can he be blamed for bitterly resenting the trick played on him by Pompilia's ignoble parents?

With the cunning of an excellent story-teller Browning gradually demolishes our credulity about Franceschini. We hear Caponsacchi, the priest. Can we believe that this handsome, cultivated, worldly young man, known for the slackness of his vows, came to desire the salvation and not the seduction of Pompilia? But we know our Browning by now, the "cosmic detective" nosing out virtue in our unlikeliest moments; and though Pompilia's lawyer appears to be much fonder of his diction than careful of the interest of his client, we know that the unravelling of motive and evidence will eventually lead to her innocence. Her simple story comes from her own lips, artless and pathetic, as she dies. One more of those Victorian innocents, fragile, wraith-like, childish, affecting at their best, sickly at their worst, breathes her last in the Victorian phantasmagoria where ogre-like villains and corrupted worldings nudge and snarl together in the smoke. How they liked suffering in women.

The realism, Browning's eye for the physical, conveys an extraordinary excitement. He cannot describe an emotion or sensation without putting a hat and coat on it:

> Till sudden at the door a tap discreet
> A visitor's premonitory cough,
> And poverty has reached him on her rounds.

Or

> . . . Guido woke
> After the cuckoo, so late, near noon day
> With an inordinate yawning of the jaws,
> Ears plugged, eyes gummed together, palate, tongue
> And teeth one mud-paste made of poppy milk.

Or

> The brother walking misery away
> O' the mountain side with dog and gun belike.

His people live, their thoughts live physically; indeed they live so physically that in the metaphors they breed a crowd of other things and other people, cramming the narrative until the main theme is blocked and obscured. A stuttering demagogue, said Chesterton. A crowd of thoughts, arguments, theories, casuistries, images, doubts and aspirations, in physical shape, are trying to get to the point of Browning's pen all at once and they reduce him to illegibility.

The Ring and the Book of the seventies has become *The Waste Land* of to-day. The Browning bric-à-brac, the

Browning personalities, the "points of view", the arguments, have degenerated into a threadbare remnant:

"These fragments I have shored against my ruins."

Shantih, shantih, the end of individualism and free speech. When one reads the heirs of Browning and especially the subjective, personal and obscure poets with their private worlds, their family jokes, their shop talk and code language, one sees what their work has lost in interest and meaning by the lack of that framework of dramatic realism which gives the cogency of event to Browning's poems. There is a reason for this loss. Private life in the nineteenth century had its public sanction; nowadays private life is something which we live against the whole current of our time. For the moment.

THE FIRST AND LAST OF HARDY

How little a novelist's choice of story and character widens or changes between his first book and his last. In an obvious way there seems to be no kinship between Hardy's *Under the Greenwood Tree* and *Jude the Obscure*, but reading these books again we see their differences are on the surface. Only age separates the youthful pastoral from the middle-aged tract. One is the sapling, pretty in its April leafage, the other is the groaning winter oak, stark with argument; but the same bitter juice rises in both their stems. Sue Bridehead is one of the consequences of being Fancy Day, Jude is a Dick Dewy become conscious of his obscurity; the tantalised youth has become the frustrated man and, according to such biographical notes as I have seen, all is a variation on the theme of Hardy's first marriage. What has changed, of course, is the stretch of the scene. After the *Greenwood Tree*, we are always struck by the largeness of the panorama and by the narrowness of Hardy's single, crooked, well-trodden path across it. And if the path is narrow, so is the man. He stands like a small, gaitered farmer in his field, dry, set, isolated and phlegmatic, the most unlikely exponent of human passion, but somehow majestic because he is on the skyline.

There have been dozens of English rural novels like *Under the Greenwood Tree*, there have been none at all like the rest of Hardy's work. He is the only English novelist who knows what the life, speech and values of the cottager really are and who knows them from the inside. Unlike the urban novelists he is not secretly laughing at the countryman, nor blatantly poeticising him. From an urban point of view, indeed, Hardy is totally unpoetic. His verse, his prose and what poetic feeling he has, are as awkward as the jerking and jangling of plough and harrow. Where, to the urban writer, the poetry of the countryside and the countryman lies in the sight of natural beauty and a feeling that here life is as sweet and sound as an apple, to Hardy the beauty is as bitter as grass. The native reek of shag and onions seems to come off his people's breath. You have the sense that these people work and work for wages. And they speak like peasants, too, a speech which is not pure decorative dialect—the weakness of the poetic novelists who have tried to do for England what Synge did for the West of Ireland—but a mixture of dialect and the trite, sententious domestic phrase.

In rescuing the dying peasant of the empty and derelict countryside from cultured sentiment, Hardy put him where Burns and Piers Plowman had found him. Yet Hardy did not achieve this by giving up all outside standards and by attempting to merge spiritually with the peasant in the manner of modern mystical writers like Giono. So far from doing this, Hardy is even something of the Victorian antiquary who smacks of the local museum. His view of man is geological. What he did was not to merge but indeed to step aside from his subject and to look at the peasant again from the point of view of the characteristic thought of his day. Hardy is unique among Victorian novelists in this sense: he is not our first novelist to be influenced by scientific ideas—there was Swift—but he is the only Victorian novelist to have been influenced by them. He seems to be the only English novelist to have read his Darwin and, like Zola who had also done so, to have had his imagination enlarged, not by the moral conflicts which Darwinism started among English writers, but by the most striking material contribution of Darwinism to our minds: its enormous widening of our conception of time. A huge and dramatic new vista was added to the years and an emancipated imagination was now free to march beyond the homely Christian fables on to the bleak and endless plain of human history. Where other writers were left to struggle with their religious faith and were gradually to lose it or to compromise in the rather woolly world of "Christian values", Hardy's imagination was stimulated to re-create the human ritual. Only in *Jude*, at the end of his career as a novelist, do we see that he, too, may have had his moral struggle with orthodox Christianity, but it seems quickly to have been settled. The very timidity of Hardy's nature, so obvious in every page, gave him a personal loneliness, an instinct to go more than half-way to accept the worst, and these readily made acceptable the great indifferent *It* and the long empty, frightening Eons of *It's* life. In the competitive stampede of Victorian liberty the peasant was left behind, he was not the fittest to survive; under the iron stamp of Hardy's Victorian determinism, he became fixed, lonely and great.

This is said to be the weakness and not the strength of Hardy. And it is true that a novelist is usually ruined by his philosophy of life. Easily shown to be untenable, a philosophy is also easily shown to be the element by which an art and human nature are falsified. The world is not a machine. Knowing this and, under the influence of French and Russian novelists, and with the decline, too, of self-confidence in middle-class culture, the English novelist has tried letting life tell its own story or, as in the case of D. H. Lawrence, has made heavy borrowings from exotic cultures. When we compare the result of this with Hardy's achievement, our position is humiliating. Whatever else the English novel may have achieved during the last thirty years, it has not described English life. It has described the sensibility of Western cosmopolitana and has been the work of people who have been, essentially, expatriates in their own country. There is, of course, a curious passage in *Jude*, after the murder of the children, when the doctor wonders whether the unrest growing in society has not awakened a universal wish for death, a passage which shows that the disintegrating ferment was working in Hardy himself. But his beliefs were cast in the sober, native moralistic mould. Since Puritanism we have always had this worried gravity and our moral instinct has been social and practical, not intellectual. When we open Hardy again we are back to worry and moral conflict, the normal condition of the English nature. The nerves relax as we prepare for what in our bones we understand: liberty loved chiefly when manacled to an inordinate respect for circumstance, the cry of passion almost silenced by windy ruminations over right and wrong. The very prose of Hardy, heavy with a·latinity which suggests a Milton reborn to drive a steamroller along the Wessex roads, has the effect of pressing men down among their neighbours and into the hills and towns where they live. Around the "rages of the ages" assembles the rural district council and, beyond that body, a moral hierarchy of which the council is the awkward shadow. As in Ibsen, Fate works, with a revived gusto, among the sanitary engineers.

In the pastoral realism of *Under the Greenwood Tree* there is a visual vividness, despite some old-fashioned phrasing, which is what we especially like today and the talk of the cottagers is taken, rich and crooked, as it comes from their mouths. If one discards the quaint scenes when the Mellstock worthies are together, there are passages which have the true, unpolished country look, in the plain comedy of Fancy's wedding at the end. The tranter is speaking of his marriage:

> "Ay, 'twas a White Tuesday when I committed it. Mellstock Club walked the same day and we new-married folk went a-gaying round the parish behind 'em. Everybody used to wear something white at Whitsuntide in them days. My sonnies, I've got the very white trousers that I wore at home in a box now. Ha'n't I, Ann?"
> "You had till I cut 'em up for Jimmy," said Mrs. Dewy.

But long before *Jude*, the visual brightness had gone. There appeared instead that faculty of instant abstraction in Hardy's eye, whereby the people, the towns, the country, became something generalised in the mind as if Time had absorbed them. The light catches the vanes of Christminster and they glint the more brightly because they are seen against an abstract foreground "of secondary and tertiary hues". One is looking at things not seen by an eye but known by a mind, by tens of thousands of minds. If society in the mass could see, if a town or village could look, this is what they would see. Masses themselves, they would see beyond the surface to the mass beneath. The realism of Hardy is a realism of mass, you are aware all the time that hundreds of other people are passing and bumping into Jude and Sue Bridehead when they stand in the street or go to the train, carrying their passion with them. They are tired, not fired, by passion. It is something which has come out of the inherited human destiny, to use them. Jude confesses to his first marriage in a vegetable market, he is seen by his first wife in the crowd at an Agricultural Show. In streets, on railway platforms, in lodging houses, inns and empty churches, his tragedy is enacted. The fidelity of Hardy's descriptions of love-affairs does not really lie in his evocation of love itself, which is not especially good, but of its circumstances. The characters of Hardy, being rural people, are always on small local journeys, trailing their lives about with them, printing their history fragmentarily as they go upon vehicles and roads. Where the modern novelist uses journeys as a device in which, perhaps, to go into his characters' thoughts or to pick up scenes from the past, in Hardy the journeys themselves are tragic because they are bound into the business of his characters. The humdrum circumstance becomes a kind of social poetry. Hardy himself called it "the low, sad music of humanity".

The chief criticism of Hardy's technique as a novelist usually falls upon his use of coincidence, melodrama and fateful accidental meetings. He is said to overload the dice. Now the question of melodrama in Victorian life and fiction is not anything like as simple as it looks—I discuss this point later in dealing with Mrs. Gaskell's novels about industrial unrest—but certain distinctions must be made. For example, the accidental meetings of Jude with his first wife after they have parted for years seem to me not only artistically permissible but, given Hardy's method, artistically desirable. We happen nowadays to be less interested than he in the irony of circumstance; our irony is altogether satirical. By it we disparage our characters personally because we are criticising their standards and behaviour. In Hardy there is no personal disparagement. He hates no one, disapproves of very few people. The disparagement—and it is all the more true and shattering because of this—comes not from a superior author but from the triviality of the circumstances in which people live. An Agricultural Show, the mere changing of trains at a junction, may start the poison in high human feeling. We are mocked by *things*; things themselves are but the expression of "It". We rightly object to this kind of coincidence in the cheap romantic literature of wishes, in them the convention is mechanical and worn out. In Hardy, on the other hand, coincidence is far from being the unreal literary trick of a commercial story-teller; such mechanism falls naturally into place in his mechanistic philosophy.

Far indeed from suffering from coincidence Hardy is the master of coincidence. He is its master because he is the master of the movement of people. What are the scenes we most vividly remember? They are, I think, the journeys. The whole burden of the story weighs upon them. The tragic idea of people circling further and further from the crux of their fate and yet mile by mile coming inescapably nearer to it, is very familiar; Hardy fills in the provincial detail of this conception. Again, it is not tragic feeling which is his subject, but the burden of feeling. At a high moment like the murder of the children in *Jude*, Hardy completely fails to convince or move us, and this is not only because the whole episode is too much in itself; the failure owes something to the fact that in the preceding pages which describe how Jude and Sue are turned out of one lodging after another in Christminster, either because they are unmarried or because they have noisy children, Hardy has described something far more real, more fated and more significant.

As so many Victorian novels do, *Jude* suffers at crucial moments from the intervention of the author. "The poor fellow," we are told, "poor Jude", "honest Jude", and so on. When a novelist pities a prig he is usually writing about himself and Jude walks stiffly and bookishly to his doom. Cynical critics have pointed out that if Jude had been born a little later he would have gone to Ruskin College and the whole tragedy would not have happened. This is a nonsensical criticism. There *is* a tragedy of the desire for knowledge. Hardy's analysis of the phases of Jude's intellectual development and disillusion is masterly and only fails when he makes Jude die with the bells of Remembrance Day at Christminster in his ears. That is as bad as the lovers kissing under the gibbet where ten years later one of them will be hanged. The reason, to my mind, why the book fails, is that part of it is a tract on the marriage laws. It would have been perfectly fitting for Jude to be ruined by two women, one a sensual slut and the other a fey, half-sexed coquette posing as a creature of fastidious higher nature, without dragging the marriage laws in. Hardy was at his worst in attacking convention, because his interests were so narrow. What are his tragedies? Love stories only, the enormous Victorian preoccupation with sex. He seems never to have outgrown the tantalisation, the frustration which the Sue Brideheads brought down upon their husbands, making them expert, as only the true Puritan can be, on the pathetic subject of female vanity. So obsessed, the Victorians could never turn easily from sex to other dramas around them—as Zola could turn to the mines and the soil, Balzac to money, Dickens to the farces and tragedies of the law. The attack upon convention is one of the great bores of the late Victorian period, for all the attackers except Shaw thought they could get rid of conventions without altering the basis of the kind of society which produced them.

A CURATE'S DIARY

A WRITER'S humiliations come at every hour of the day and one of the greatest is the common failure of professional authors to write an interesting diary. Most of them try. The thing looks so easy, so indolent a labour, so casual and go-as-you-please. No shape to torture, no plot to drive one mad, no scheme to follow. One looks out of the window with an empty mind and lets the day pour in its news like the varieties of light coming in from the garden. Or so it seems. Yet, let the professional writer compare his jottings with those of the famous diarists. Let him look at Amiel or Pepys, Woodforde or Evelyn, and the discrepancy is shattering. Why such a coarseness of texture, such a failure in intimacy, even such an absence of newsiness? Obviously diary writing is *not* an affair of the idle moment, *not* a spare-time occupation. It must be a life-work, one's only literary work, one of the constant domestic arts like gossip, cookery or gardening which leave little mind for anything else. The diary is indeed the revenge of the secretive and of the failures upon the public self-importance of the world of letters. A mere schoolmaster, a piffling clergyman, an official limpet, may jump at once to permanent fame without the agony of an author's vanity.

And of course without an author's rewards. The one consolation to the regular professionals is that no diarist reaches fame in his own lifetime. He sows but he does not reap. We have had a recent example of this poetic injustice in the case of the Reverend Kilvert. We cannot know what this shy, gracious and strangely ecstatic Victorian curate would have thought if he had known that the eyes of the public would one day swarm like flies over the three volumes of his private diary. Perhaps he would have been pleased and had half hoped to be read. For it seems very doubtful that a man, who takes an obvious trouble to write well, should do so entirely for himself. There must be, one feels, a limit to the satisfactions of self-love; and Kilvert had that Victorian sense of duty or responsibility which would give him the need of an object for his daily record. He was very much aware of recording history, if only with a small "h" and he cannot have been so different from his contemporaries who lived in a society so set and with such an air of eternity about its conventions, practices and beliefs, that they regarded themselves as a kind of communal phenomenon. That sense of belonging to a society is one which has been lost in the last thirty years—hence the awful fuss we make about it to-day when we try to set down our beliefs, speaking of it as something distant, revolutionary, Utopian—and it was that sense which made Kilvert an historian.

Diary writing is the most private of the arts. It is not really surprising therefore that the Wiltshire and Radnorshire curate should have stopped writing before his marriage. In any case he could not have experimented in the difficult task of combining diary keeping with marriage, for he died a month later. Privacy was going. For some time he had been too busy with marriage preparations to write many of those long lyrical entries of the earlier pages. We feel indeed that a phase had finished. Kilvert had given the best of himself and though his death was tragically sudden, he died, from a literary point of view, at the right time—at one of the two or three right times which a talented man has in his life.

What would marriage and family life have done to the innocent ardours of this susceptible bachelor? A difficult time, we suspect, awaited the lyrical idealist who was put in "a state of continual bewitchment" (as Mr. Plomer, his editor, says), and "emotional upheaval" by every female he met, child, girl or young woman. A wife might not have understood this "strange and terrible gift of stealing hearts and exciting such love" which was an instinct of his rapturous nature. And how rapturous it was! The little deaf and dumb girl who flings her arms round him makes him cry out, "I have been loved; no one can take this from me". An Irish girl sends him into ecstasy with her play-acting on a train journey. There are Ettie and "the wild, mad trysts in the snow". There is a procession of girls and girl children with "glorious" hair or "glorious" eyes and hosts of chaste but exciting kissings, as if his heart were a spring day. We love by the book and Kilvert had read his Tennyson; but it is the special triumph of Kilvert's sincerity that he has conveyed and made credible his kind of feeling to a generation whose notions of love are totally alien to those of a bubbling young mid-Victorian curate:

> How delightful it is in these sweet summer evenings to wander from cottage to cottage and from farm to farm exchanging bright words and looks with the beautiful girls at their garden gates and talking to the kindly people sitting at their cottage doors or meeting in the lane when their work is done. How sweet it is to pass from house to house welcome and beloved everywhere by young and old, to meet the happy loving smile of the dear children at their evening play in the lanes and fields and to meet with no harsher reproach than this. "It is a longful while since you have been to see us. We do all love to see you coming and we do miss you sorely when you are away."

We have lost the art of rendering pure sentiment and the feeling for such a tenderness as Kilvert's. Echoes of the stage clergyman—"the deah children"—run mocking along the lines as we read a passage like that. But Kilvert's *Diary* might be called the revenge of the comic curate. His sensibility and dignity show up the Edwardian horseplay at the expense of the clergy for the dated boorishness it is. When we contrast the note and rhythm of our lives with those of Kilvert's we see there is more than a change of fashions between the generations. We perceive with a shock that it is we who are unnatural because we do not live within the walls of a long period of civilisation and peace. It is we who are the abnormal, distorted people: creatures of a revolutionary age who of all human types are the most passagery, and least characteristic, the most ill-fitting and bizarre.

Towards the end of his short life Kilvert was in Wiltshire acting as curate to his father. An account of Kilvert's father who kept a school during his son's earliest childhood, is to be found in Augustus Hare's autobiography. Hare wrote: "at nine years old I was compelled to eat Eve's apple quite up; indeed the Tree of Knowledge of Good and Evil was stripped absolutely bare: there was no fruit left to gather". Was Kilvert's prolonged and limpid innocence the result of some early check of horror? There is one incident in the third volume which catches the prying eye of the modern reader and which makes him hesitate about that innocence. There would be no hesitation but for the fact that Kilvert's virginal innocence is phenomenal. At 38 it is a major feat of clerical sublimation. The incident concerns a village girl who had become hopelessly disobedient and uncontrollable. She had been reasoned with, prayed over, punished without result. There was nothing for it, Kilvert said, but formally and solemnly to give her a good whipping and he offered to do it for the parents. The offer was refused but it was agreed to allow him to be present. There may be nothing in it. Kilvert records it exactly as he records any other village happening; but it gives one a shock, for he had no cruelty in his nature. The shock does not arise from the act alone. What shakes us is that, charmed by the Victorian felicity, we had forgotten for a moment the price the Victorians paid for their ignorance of themselves.

There was nothing spinsterly in Kilvert; his sensibility is masculine, or as the Victorians would have said "manly". After Wiltshire Kilvert went to the Border country once more where he was always happiest. He responded to the lively imaginative and courteous Welsh people. The Border country provides many of his best characters. In Wiltshire the comedy is heavier. There was the row about Mrs. Prodgers, for example; there was the campaign which raged between the vicar and the squire about the harmonium. And then so many of those little girls who jumped up to kiss the curate would suddenly die. The diary form lends itself even better than the novel or the short tale to rounding off character, for life is always adding its felicitous afterthought. Where art is selective and one-sided, the diary dips its net daily and brings out what is there. Take the Prodgers incident. Mrs. Prodgers was one of those pushful, fecund and importunate parishioners who bring their umbrellas down with a firm tap on every vicarage doorstep. She came from Kingston St. Michael, a village where droll things were always happening, and caused a lot of tittering when she insisted that she and the little Prodgers should be used as models in the design of the new stained-glass window for the church. "Suffer the little children" was the subject, and Mrs. Prodgers had edged her brood of sufferers well into the foreground of the picture. Doubly immortal Mrs. Prodgers to be done both by Kilvert and by stained glass. In a few lines there is the essence of a life-story. It is not worth more, it is not worth less. Outside a stained-glass window, a diary note is the perfect place for her. And then the Squire. He illustrates the aptitude of the diary form for collecting fragments day by day, for catching each day's contribution to the jig-saw of human character. The novelist must summarise, theorise and jump to conclusions; the diarist can take the more leisurely course of letting the character out piecemeal, as he makes himself. A vicar-baiter and a tyrant, the Squire ordered the tenor to be turned out of the choir and so spoiled the singing, but opposed "with strong language" the proposal to introduce a harmonium. "Distant from music" was one woman's description of him. "He apprehended", he said, "a chronic difficulty in finding someone to play the instrument." The Kilverts won, but the Squire wouldn't pay a penny. That is not the end of the Squire. His portrait is perfected a few days later in the midst of a later and very affecting description of a child's funeral. Kilvert, familiar with rural sorrow and intensely observant, had a perceptiveness uncommon in literature. We see the mother's distracted face, her cries of guilt and helplessness, her hard, despairing eye. And then the afternoon sun shines in the church and the birds begin to sing as if in honour of the dead child and Kilvert, as he reads the service, catches sight of the Squire through the window. He is dressed in a white hat and a drab suit, dashing fussily across the churchyard and putting his stick into the grave to see that it is the right depth. Things must be done properly.

Kilvert has always these completing realistic touches so that a scene is never made top-heavy with the emotion it arouses. His eye and ear are acute; they seem always to be roving over the scene and to hit upon some sight or word which is all the more decisive for having the air of accident. And in literature, to convey the chance effects of life without being bizarre is everything. So he goes on his walking tours, has his holidays in Sussex, the Isle of Wight, marks his catalogue at Burlington House, loses his easy heart, preaches, consoles the sick, collecting the odd but never isolating it from the stream of living in the manner of the caricaturist. An old lady—you could meet her in the town if you wanted—was parachuted over the cliff hanging from her umbrella in a gale and alighted unhurt. Another "grasped at vacancy" on the cellar stairs and fell to the bottom; the trouble began when her husband at the top explained that she couldn't have done so because you can't grasp at vacancy—a grotesque bit of domestic argument. An old man on his deathbed says, "It is hard work dying," and a fine farmer wrecked by illness in middle life says sadly, "I shall never again be a big man like you with your strong body." These things are too sharp when detached from Kilvert's context; in that, they are the windows of a way of rural life which is far from gone, though curates go no more to drink whey with dairymaids or dance Roger de Coverley at picnics with the prettiest girls of the parish.

Kilvert's account of his visit to Priscilla Price shows him at his dramatic best. The old lady was 77 and could remember the coronation of George IV. She lived with her step-daughter, a woman turned 50 who was an idiot. They were an astonishing pair, for the idiot added a touch of frightening parody to the picture. They were drinking tea in their cottage when Kilvert found them. What an excellent short story they make:

"Ar Tader, Ar Tader!" cried the idiot. "She means 'Our Father'," explained the stepmother. " She has been wanting to see the clergyman, the gentleman that says 'Our Father'." Prissy detailed to me the story of an illness she had suffered, illustrated by a dramatic performance by the idiot as a running accompaniment. Occasionally in addition to the acting of the details of the illness, the bursting of a blood vessel, the holding of the head of the invalid, and yelling to the neighbours for help, the idiot roared out an affirmative or negative according to the requirements of the tale. "The blood spouted up," said Prissy. "Yes," thundered the idiot. "She held my head," explained Prissy. "Yes," roared the idiot. "There was no one here but her," said Prissy. "No"! shouted the idiot. "They say that Mr. Davies heard her crying for help as far as Fine Street," declared Prissy. "Yes!" asseverated the idiot with a roar of pride and satisfaction. "She had to run out into the deep snow," said the stepmother. The idiot stepdaughter measured the depth of the snow upon her thigh.

Later Kilvert was asked to read the Testament and pray:

The reading was accompanied by a running fire of ejaculations and devout utterances from Prissy. She put a mat on the floor for me to kneel on and knelt down herself with some pain and difficulty, having sprained her knee. I begged her to be seated. "No," she said. "I will kneel. I must punish the body. Kneel down, my dear," she said reprovingly to the idiot. The idiot knelt humbly down in front of the fire with her head almost in the ashes.

There were other meetings like this. Priscilla collected old lore. She told the story of a man at Staunton-by-Wye who had seen the oxen kneel down at midnight on Christmas Eve and stay there moaning, the tears running down their faces.

Those especially Victorian words, words which bring back a whole period: "radiant, glorious, infinite, innocence, picturesque," are common in Kilvert's descriptions of scenery or of his sentiment. "A splendid romp with Polly Taverner"— that is an authentic note from the time. His broken romances belong to the period too. Where Kilvert is superior to many of the novelists is that he is writing straight from nature, idealising often but never falsifying, for he moralises very little. His piety like his sentiment is firm but unprofessional. A being who feels, he does not go into the muddy introspections which many diary writers love, he has humour but he does not make insincere, defensive diary jokes against himself. One likes him in the end, I am convinced, because entirely without self importance or self-consciousness, he is serious about himself. That supremely difficult art! Putting those three volumes down, one reflects that too many diarists are not content to work within a small field. A diary needs a frame and they are not willing to make it anything less than the universe. It is a pity, for the village is more interesting.

THE GREAT FLUNKEY

JUDGED by their portraits, what a large number of the Victorian writers seem not to be writers at all, but creatures
trom the Green Room and the stage! There are the haggard,
Irving-like grimaces of Dickens, the dank, baleful ringlets, so
Siddonish, of George Eliot and Elizabeth Barrett. Tennyson
glowers like the bearded villain from the Lyceum. They
were a histrionic generation and in a way the habit embellishes
them. But not all. Every prejudice we feel about Thackeray
is confirmed by his disastrous portraits. Did ever a snob look
more like a footman, was ever a man of the world more easily
mistaken—as so often occurs to men of the world—for one
of the servants? Take the very literary steel spectacles from
Thackeray's nose in Samuel Lawrence's portrait, and what is
more damning than that episcopal look of his, as if he were
at once a bishop, bland and patronising, at a ducal christening,
and Mr. Yellowplush himself announcing in the long soirée
of Victorian letters, that the carriage has arrived? What a
rôle to have chosen—to be the great flunkey of God and
Mammon, the whited expert on the whited sepulchres.

There is, naturally, more in the portrait than that. Bishops
and footmen have not that sensibility; his eyes have not the
vacant stare of servitude; and the chin, which Thackeray
raises so high, seems to be raised defensively rather than super-
ciliously. Like an actor's, it suggests the pride of a personal
style. People who knew Thackeray well said that they had
never got to the bottom of him, and one can well believe
it. One is held off. And yet one cannot escape him. Other
novelists conceal themselves, but the figure of Thackeray is

pushed forward in advance of his characters. We simply have to make up our minds about him personally because in all those novels "without a hero" he is the hero himself, the compère of his own show. We are obliged to know the flow of his egoism better than we shall know the Osbornes and the Sedleys or any of his characters.

Re-reading *Vanity Fair* again, one realises what a brilliant innovation this was in the English novel. *Vanity Fair* is, as the traditional usually turns out to be, a new experiment. A new experiment in the manner of Sterne. Before everything, Thackeray was a versatile journalist, the author of clever sketches and short pieces which are still sharp and pungent in their satire after three generations. Egoistical but detached, he is alive to the current of life, the stream on which the curious fragments called human beings are borne. He observes. He does not appear to have a sustained imaginative power which can create a character larger than life, like one of Balzac's, though his interests resemble Balzac's. (He has more in common with Balzac than with Dickens.) Thackeray is like the modern novelists who derive from James and Proust, in his power of dissecting (and of desiccating!) character, in the refusal to inflate it. For a Victorian, we feel this had to be a fatal originality. The long novel, the great theme, the crowded canvas, were essential. Thackeray can see this, yet he must realise that his genius is for the fragmentary. And so he disguises his inability to create the proper paraphernalia of fiction, by introducing himself as the *raconteur*, who, having got you to listen, can distract, delude and beguile you with an atmosphere—an atmosphere which lifts like a haze from time to time upon one of those interludes of real talk, action and character which are as true as life itself. A voice talks on, going forward, winding backward, playing with scene and time. We see that this is not merely a new kind of narrative, but that Thackeray catches the illusion of living as none of his contemporaries ever did. They were inclined too much to be interested in the outsize thing called Life.

Another innovation—and Thackeray seems always to be innovating—is his attitude of character. There are no fixed characters in *Vanity Fair*. Amelia, Becky, that grim wreck Miss Crawley, the egotistical young soldier, George Osborne, old Sedley the virtuous bankrupt, and Jos, his son, the Regency dandy and glutton—they are not defined once and for all. They change with the story, they change in time, their view of one another changes. Thackeray makes them fluid and unexpected. It is a wicked concession to melodrama and humbug that Becky apparently murders Jos Sedley at the end. And yet, what is more perfect than the career of this buffoon? Comically drunk at Vauxhall at the beginning, then respectably in flight from his errors, he turns up dressed for the part in Brussels before Waterloo. Then panic again. Clothes, "dashed fine gals and ices" become the ruling passions of this windy, fat and simple hypochondriac. Food-poisoning in low company is the fitting end, even if it is incredible that Becky had been studying Jos Sedley's liver all these years in order to commit the crime. Becky and Rawdon are greater examples of Thackeray's eye for the unexpected in character. It is a pity that Thackeray had to preach to us about Becky for, whether taking her side or not, he was capable of letting her live for herself. The stay at Crawley, when she is received into the family and listens to Lady Southdown's homilies, winds the wool and sings Haydn in the evenings, is made perfect by Becky's pleasure in it. It is a brief pleasure, for Becky is no fool. "I could be good", she reflects, "if I had £5,000 a year." Then again there is Rawdon, the brainless Guardsman, the "Mayfair playboy" with "no harm" in him. His famous bequest of his horse to Becky as he goes off to battle, is the crown of stumbling humanity upon his character:

"Look here," said he. "If I drop, let us see what there

is for you. I have had a pretty good run of luck here, and here's two hundred and thirty pounds. I have got two Napoleons in my pocket. That is as much as I shall want; for the General pays everything like a prince; and if I'm hit, why you know I cost nothing. Don't cry, little woman; I may live to vex you yet. Well, I shan't take either of my horses, but shall ride the General's grey charger; it's cheaper, and I told him mine was lame. If I'm done, those two ought to fetch you something. Grigg offered ninety for the mare yesterday, before this confounded news came, and like a fool I wouldn't let her go under the two 0's. Bullfinch will fetch his price any day, only you'd better sell him in this country, because the dealers have so many bills of mine, and so I'd rather he shouldn't go back to England. Your little mare the General gave you will fetch something, and there's no d——d livery-stable bills here, as there are in London," Rawdon added with a laugh. "There's that dressing-case cost me two hundred —that is, I owe two for it; and the gold tops and bottles must be worth thirty or forty. Please to put *that* up the spout, ma'am, with my pins and rings, and watch and chain, and things. They cost a precious lot of money. Miss Crawley, I know, paid a hundred down for the chain and ticker. Gold tops and bottles, indeed! dammy. I'm sorry I didn't take more now. Edwards pressed on me a silver-gilt boot-jack, and I might have had a dressing-case fitted up with a silver warming-pan, and a service of plate. But we must make the best of what we've got, Becky, you know."

And so, making his last dispositions, Captain Crawley, who had seldom thought about anything but himself until the last few months of his life, when Love had obtained the mastery over the dragoon, went through the various items of his little catalogue of effects, striving to see how they might be turned into money for his wife's benefit, in case any accident should befall him. He pleased himself by noting down with a pencil, in his big schoolboy handwriting, the various items of his portable property which might be sold for his widow's advantage—as, for example, "My double-barril by Manton, say 40 guineas; my driving cloak, lined with sable fur, £50; my duelling pistols in rosewood case (same which I shot Captain Marker) £20; my regulation saddle-holsters and housings; my Laurie ditto" and so forth, over all of which articles he made Rebecca the mistress.

Faithful to his plan of economy, the Captain dressed himself in his oldest and shabbiest uniform and epaulets, leaving the newest behind under his wife's (or it might be his widow's) guardianship. And this famous dandy of Windsor and Hyde Park went off on his campaign with a kit as modest as that of a sergeant, and with something like a prayer on his lips for the woman he was leaving. He took her up from the ground, and held her in his arms for a minute, tight pressed against his strong-beating heart. His face was purple and his eyes dim as he put her down and left her. He rode by his General's side, and smoked his cigar in silence as they hastened after the troops of the General's brigade, which preceded them; and it was not until they were some miles on their way that he left off twirling his mustachio and broke silence.

The virtue of such incidents is not merely their comedy; it is their reality. With every line in these portraits—and, I say, in the portraits not in the disquisitions Thackeray wrote under them—there is an extension of reality, the excitement of the detective who goes from clue to clue. And still the honeymoon at Brighton with Becky being witty about the moon while her husband sharps at cards in the room behind her, and the Brussels chapters, stand out as a culminating height in English comic writing. The bullet in George Osborne's heart is not so good; but the rest—well, in the first year of this war we saw the whole Thackerean scene enacted again.

Thackeray and Balzac: they are like the opposite sides of the same penny. Here is young George Osborne speaking to Amelia:

"Ours is a ready money society. We live among bankers
and city big-wigs, and be hanged to them, and every man as
he talks to you jingles his guineas in his pocket."

Money in Balzac is as dynamic as a passion; in Thackeray
it is less massive; it is as ubiquitous as the senses. True, it
is reduced in his philosophy to the common level of vanity,
another factor which the moralist washes down with another
glass of vintage sadness; but in the narrative Thackeray understands money and its place in the contemporary situation.
Waterloo must have looked romantic in 1840, yet Thackeray
also knew who won that battle. It is not an accident that
Osborne and Sedley are Stock Exchange speculators, the newest
representatives of middle-class finance. And in the cut-throat
stage, too. He knows the anxiety of the aristocracy—"make
them pay up first and cut them afterwards"—and the anxiety
of speculators to get their sons and daughters into the class
above them. Thackeray's picture of the Regency aristocracy
is a caricature, as we know from the memoirs of the time;
it is a middle-class view which understands the aristocrats only
when, like Lady Southdown, they catch the infection of middle-
class piety. But how proper is the distinction he makes between the attitude of the various members of the Crawley
family to Miss Crawley's fortune, and the attitude of old
Osborne to *his* fortune. The portrait of Miss Crawley—the
greatest character in the book to my mind—makes one wonder
if Thackeray did always go wrong about aristocrats. (I take
it she was one? An old-fashioned revolutionary aristocrat,
already an anachronism before Waterloo.) She is the one
character who understands Becky, and it is the older, shrewder
feeling of her generation for money which sharpens Miss
Crawley's eyes. One seems to see wills becoming deeds, deeds
becoming notes, notes dissolving into coins and passing from
above from hand to hand until they reach the dress-wiping
palms of the servants, in nearly every page of this novel. It

was a perception which was no doubt heightened in Thackeray by the taboo on sex; so that socially the background is perfect, where the individuals are castrated.

One does not say that the inability to write about love as a sexual passion is fatal to a novelist; but in Thackeray the people do become, as he says, "Puppets". They are small to the eye, figures seen through the wrong end of a telescope. As egotists, they are made mean by their sexlessness; for there is a generosity about sexual egotism. We recall the terrible crime of Becky, even in her schooldays: "she was old in life and experience". After the hush caused by that remark, we do not to-day rise, as we were intended to do, to nobler heights; on the contrary, we sink to that plane where the "quid" dominates its unmentionable partnership with the "pro quo".

But the pleasure of Thackeray is in the sense of Style, in the intimacy with an educated mind. It is absurd to condemn the educated for being humbugs: they are merely more skilful humbugs. Since when have the educated been observed to "know better", to be any more than a more self-conscious product of their times? Remove the vices of a novelist and his virtues vanish too. To us, and especially since the two wars, Thackeray is the great sedentary novelist, a moralist to whom adventure and physical action are alien; and that cuts him off. He is cut off by his melancholy—a peacetime luxury: our emotion is sharp, dramatic and tragic. But in *Vanity Fair*, in those hundreds of fragmentary pictures where scenes are crystallised and people talk, there is the original journalist Thackeray. Here are Rawdon and Becky again, first Thackeray the compère, then the reporter:

An article as necessary to a lady in this position as her brougham or her bouquet, is her companion. I have always admired the way in which the tender creatures, who cannot exist without sympathy, hire an exceedingly plain friend of their own sex from whom they are almost inseparable. The sight of that inevitable woman in her faded gown seated behind her dear friend in the opera-box, or occupying the back seat of the barouche, is always a wholesome and moral one to me, as jolly a reminder as that of the Death's-head which figured in the repasts of Egyptian *bons vivants*, a strange sardonic memorial of Vanity Fair. What?—even battered, brazen, beautiful conscienceless, heartless Mrs. Firebrace, whose father died of her shame; even lovely, daring Mrs. Mantrap, who will ride at any fence which any man in England will take, and who drives her greys in the Park, while her mother keeps a huckster's stall in Bath still;—even those who are so bold, one might fancy they could face anything, dare not face the world without a female friend. They must have somebody to cling to, the affectionate creatures! And you will hardly see them in any public place without a shabby companion in a dyed silk, sitting somewhere in the shade close behind them.

"Rawdon", said Becky, very late one night, as a party of gentlemen were seated round her crackling drawing-room fire (for the men came to her house to finish the night; and she had ice and coffee for them, the best in London): "I must have a sheep-dog."

"A what?" said Rawdon, looking up from an écarté table

"A sheep-dog!" said young Lord Southdown. "My dear Mrs. Crawley, what a fancy! What not have a Danish dog? I know of one as big as a camel-leopard, by Jove. It would almost pull your brougham. Or a Persian greyhound, eh? (I propose, if you please); or a little pug that would go into one of Lord Steyne's snuff-boxes? There's a man at Bayswater got one with such a nose that you might—I mark the king and play,—that you might hang your hat on it."

"I mark the trick," Rawdon gravely said. He attended to his game commonly, and didn't much meddle with the conversation except when it was about horses and betting.

"What *can* you want with a shepherd's dog?" the lively little Southdown continued.

"I mean a *moral* shepherd's dog," said Becky, laughing, and looking up at Lord Steyne.

"What the devil's that?" said his Lordship.

"A dog to keep the wolves off me," Rebecca continued. "A companion."

"Dear little innocent lamb, you want one," said the Marquis; and his jaw thrust out, and he began to grin hideously, his little eyes leering towards Rebecca.

The great Lord of Steyne was standing by the fire sipping coffee. The fire crackled and blazed pleasantly. There was a score of candles sparkling round the mantelpiece, in all sorts of quaint sconces, of gilt and bronze and porcelain. They lighted up Rebecca's figure to admiration, as she sate on a sofa covered with a pattern of gaudy flowers. She was in a pink dress, that looked as fresh as a rose; her dazzling white arms and shoulders were half-covered with a thin hazy scarf through which they sparkled; her hair hung in curls round her neck; one of her little feet peeped out from the fresh crisp folds of silk: the prettiest little foot in the prettiest little sandal in the finest silk stockings in the world.

The candles lighted up Lord Steyne's shining bald head, which was fringed with red hair. He had thick bushy eyebrows, with little twinkling bloodshot eyes, surrounded by a thousand wrinkles. His jaw was underhung, and when he laughed, two white buck-teeth protruded themselves and glistened savagely in the midst of the grin. He had been dining with royal personages, and wore his garter and ribbon. A short man was his Lordship, broad-chested, and bow-legged, but proud of the fineness of his foot and ankle, and always caressing his garter-knee.

"And so the Shepherd is not enough", said he, "to defend his lambkin?"

"The Shepherd is too fond of playing at cards and going to his clubs," answered Becky, laughing.

"'Gad, what a debauched Corydon!" said my Lord—"what a mouth for a pipe!"

"I take your three to two," here said Rawdon, at the card-table.

"Hark at Melibeus," snarled the noble Marquis; "he's pastorally occupied too; he's shearing a Southdown. What an innocent mutton, hey? Damme, what a snowy fleece!"

Rebecca's eyes shot out gleams of scornful humour. "My Lord," she said, "you are a knight of the Order." He had the collar round his neck, indeed—a gift of the restored Princes of Spain.

Lord Steyne in early life had been notorious for his daring and his success at play. He had sat up two days and two nights with Mr. Fox at hazard. He had won money of the most august personages of the realm; he had won his marquisate, it was said, at the gaming-table; but he did not like an allusion to those bygone *fredaines*. Rebecca saw the scowl gathering over his heavy brow.

She rose up from her sofa, and went and took his coffee-cup out of his hand with a little curtsey. "Yes," she said, "I must get a watch-dog. But he won't bark at *you*." And, going into the other drawing-room, she sat down to the piano, and began to sing little French songs in such a charming, thrilling voice, that the mollified nobleman speedily followed her into that chamber, and might be seen nodding his head and bowing time over her.

Rawdon and his friend meanwhile played écarté until they had enough. The Colonel won; but, say that he won ever so much and often, nights like these, which occurred many times in the week—his wife having all the talk and all the admiration, and he sitting silent without the circle, not comprehending a word of the jokes, the allusions, the mystical language within—must have been wearisome to the ex-dragoon.

"How is Mrs. Crawley's husband?" Lord Steyne used to say to him by way of a good-day when they met: and indeed that was now his avocation in life. He was Colonel Crawley no more. He was Mrs. Crawley's husband.

We cannot say "reporter", but how actual, on the spot, caught in the casualness of the moment, those people are. Rawdon's slang, even Jos Sedley's jokes, Becky's startling opening sentences, George Osborne's exclamations—these are not jollifications of language; they are real. *Yellowplush*, the snob book, and all those curious phonetic dialogues of his— Joyce-like in their way—indicate something like the modern ear's curiosity. Cut *Vanity Fair* by a third and the rest moves at once into step with our lives.

THE SOUTH GOES NORTH

THE chief fault of the Victorian novelists, says Lord David Cecil, writing of Mrs. Gaskell in his *Early Victorian Novelists*, is that they write beyond their range. This criticism is probably true, but it is one, I think, that must be applied with great caution. What is the range of a novelist? Even of Turgenev it has been objected that he went beyond his range in his portraits of the revolutionaries in *Virgin Soil*. There can be few novelists in any country who keep to the things they know in their bones. Opinion, beliefs collected and disputed, *weltanschauung*, are shovelled into all but the purely æsthetic novels; part of the impulse to write novels and a good deal of the material is in a sense the work of the period in which a novelist lives. It is a dangerous criticism which picks out from the past the fragments that appeal to us, and which suggests for example that the Victorian domestic charm can be separated from the Victorian sermon. And if, in picking up novels like Mrs. Gaskell's *Wives and Daughters* or *North and South*, we say we prefer a self-regarding and captivating young flirt and hedonist like Cynthia Kirkpatrick to the worthy Molly Gibsons or the prim and reprimanding Margaret Hales, we have no right to say the latter are lay figures, sticks and prigs. All early and mid-Victorian fiction, with the exception perhaps of *Wuthering Heights*, inculcates the idea of responsibility, as our own novels seek to impress us with ideas of self-sufficiency and guilt, and if *we* find responsible characters heavy going, or too good to be true, there was a time in which they were considered passionately attractive.

What a sombre, violent and emotional scene these early

Victorian novelists present. Did they create those melodramatic plots to relieve the peaceful boredom of prosperity?
A glance at the social history of the nineteenth century shows
that this cannot be so. It was a time of spiritual and material
turbulence. Victorian melodrama was only a very slightly
exaggerated picture of Victorian life. The riots, shipwrecks,
fires, lunatic asylums and deportations, we read of in the novels,
the awful family splits about legacies and estates, the sons told
never again to darken the door, the rejected lovers trekking
off to the brutal colonies, all are real enough. In these novels
one sees a panorama where women in childbed die like flies,
where stepmothers are rampant, orphanages overflow and
hordes of fallen women grovel helplessly in the wake of a
seducer who has the devil-may-care air of a disguised Sunday
School teacher. And beyond them, in the middle distance,
the factory smoke rises, the workers herd into the workshops,
the mob plunges in the streets. Everything we can learn of
Victorian life confirms the picture. People did turn out to
be the missing sons of earls, honest families *were* ruined in
the markets, clergymen *were* able to work themselves up to
crises of conscience on what seems to us a mere point of order.
My own early impression of Victorian novels in childhood
was of islands of domestic peace surrounded by a sea of moral
peril. One read not for pleasure, but to worry and to be
frightened. The truth is, I think, that a passionate and brutal
age, intoxicated above all by the idea of power—not only
Carlyle, but Mrs. Gaskell too, had a weakness for the rough
Teutonic ancestor, the Viking and the Nordic myth—could
control itself only by moral violence. The castration of youth,
the idealisation of middle age seem to indicate this. The
Victorian novel not only put the heart in the mouth; it started
the burglar alarm of conscience very loudly in the head, and
conventions are strong when the passions are strong. The
very complications of the plots and sub-plots, the stagey coinci-

dences, the impossible innocence and the impossible vice, are photographs of the Victorian mind which carried its characteristic doctrine of the survival of the fittest even into the reader's task as he sat down to be tortured into taking life still more seriously by the latest serial instalment.

It is not on these grounds that we would praise Mrs. Gaskell's *North and South* or *Mary Barton*, as the Victorian critics did; but it is on these grounds that we must defend her. They were didactic melodramas and best sellers in their time, and we must not forget this when we find *Cranford* or the social comedy of *Wives and Daughters* more to our taste.

North and South is dead now and that is a pity; for now that we have ceased to believe that the most important events in life occur only in the drawing-room, the bedroom or the psychologist's clinic, it is interesting to discover that Mrs. Gaskell was intensely moved by the questions of her time. The idea of responsibility was not merely philanthropical; it sprang from a practical and religious sense of the coherence of society.

Like all her books, except *Cranford*, like all Victorian novels, *North and South* is too long; that it is stiff, stilted and lifeless no one who has lived in the industrial North will ever agree. And on this point I must differ with Lord David Cecil. Economics were outside her range, but the men and women of the industrial revolution were not. *North and South* succeeds where Mrs. Gaskell always succeeds: in the simple essentials of character, in her skill at distinguishing and presenting manners, in her delightful eye for detail, the mild deftness of her satire. Ladylike though she was and very apt with a moral, she had an untroubled steadiness of eye when she faced human emotions. She shrank from investigating the passions, but she at least missed nothing from their outline. The motive of jealousy is lightly touched; it is never missed. Margaret Hale is a prig, no doubt, when she attacks John Thornton for abusing his workers. She is a snob also about tradesmen and manufacturers; but she is capable of strong feeling, her pride is not sick and self-consuming, but is directed outward upon her relationships with people, a firm consummate assertion of her personality. Margaret Hale is a prig, if you like, in the sense in which most of us are prigs; but it is more truthful to say that she is stubborn in her loyalties and decided in her affections. She is assured in her class, in her belief, for example, of the superiority of southern English culture when it is contrasted with the rougher manners of the North; but she has not simply inherited these things without enquiry. She has a strong mind and is prepared to argue. I take it that a novelist unwittingly draws a stick and a prig when he uses a character to express views he approves of and then, so to speak, publicly congratulates the character on being an example to us all, without building this upon the positives and negatives of human nature. Now Mrs. Gaskell is quite clear about the nature of Margaret Hale. John Thornton's dour, jealous and terrifying old mother observes Margaret with detachment and judges her as one woman judges another. Mrs. Thornton is reserved about the question of Margaret Hale's goodness; the quality the hard old lady notes with approval is not goodness; but the fundamental one of will. The plain north-country people are always quick to criticise Margaret's virtuousness. They tell her she is a mere social manner and that she fails to fulfil promises. There is, it is true, one of those awful self-sacrificial moments, so common in the early Victorian novels, when Margaret tells a lie to shield her brother. It is one of those lies which, apparently, could wreck love affairs because the Victorian belief in appearances seems to have prevented enquiry. (Obviously in a passionate age if you saw a lady walking unattended with a strange man, it was natural and stimulated more excitement if you assumed she was an abandoned woman.) Margaret Hale makes a terrible fuss about this fib of hers, treating it, in the best pious tradition, as if it were incest or adultery; but when you look at the matter more closely, you see that Mrs. Gaskell never really neglected real human motive for long. It is Margaret Hale's pride, not her conscience, which is disturbed. She is afraid that she has exposed a weakness of will to a lover whom she has so far kept at arm's length. As the portrait of a normally prim young woman (and it was Fielding who, with real Englishness, spoke of the irresistible attraction of the prude) on the defensive in a hostile environment, Mrs. Gaskell's picture of the conflicts in Margaret Hale's character is an accurate one.

John Thornton's mother is a wonderful sketch. One sees her in that too brilliant and ornate drawing-room which looks out upon the mill, a woman with a single passion, a primitive love for her son. "Her face moved slowly from one decided expression to another equally decided." Stiff and forbidding she is to the southerner, implacable, blankly insensitive and interfering, but the heart is there, now fierce, now yielding. Hard as she is, she is at her son's mercy. She is the first to see that he will fall for Margaret because of Margaret's pride, because he knows the affair will be a battle and probably will be lost. The obstinacy of the northern character, an aggressiveness in it which instinctively prefers enemies to friends, or resistance to acquiescence, is admirably displayed. This is brought out even more successfully in the tale of Thornton's relations with his workers. At first Margaret sees only the mutual hatred in the relationship; then she perceives that both sides like hating. Their hatred is a sort of independence with them, a sport, an animal instinct which on both sides seeks not moral solutions, but a master. The reconciliation of Thornton with the strike leader whom he has sacked and intends to victimise has the inevitable sugaring of Victorian domestic sentiment in it—"remember the poor children"—but it is very truthful to northern manners.

Higgins did not turn round, or immediately respond to this. But when he did speak, it was in a softened tone, although the words were gruff enough.

"Yo've no business to go prying into what happened between Boucher and me. He's dead and I'm sorry. That's enough."

"So it is. Will you take work with me? That's what I came to ask."

Higgins's obstinacy wavered, recovered strength, and stood firm. He would not speak. Mr. Thornton would not ask again. Higgins's eye fell on the children.

"Yo've called me impudent, and a liar, and a mischief-maker, and you might ha' said wi' some truth, as I were now and then given to drink. An' I ha' called you a tyrant, and an oud bull-dog, and a hard, cruel master; that's where it stands. But for th' childer. Measter, do yo' think we can e'er get on together?"

"Well!" said Mr. Thornton, half-laughing, "it was not my proposal that we should go together. But there's one comfort, on your own showing. We neither of us can think much worse of the other than we do now."

"That's true," said Higgins reflectively. "I've been thinking, ever sin' I saw you, what a marcy it were yo' did na take me on, for that I ne'er saw a man whom I could less abide. But that's maybe been a hasty judgment; and work's work to such as me. So, measter, I'll come; and what's more I thank yo'; and that's a deal fro' me," said he, more frankly, suddenly turning round and facing Mr. Thornton fully for the first time.

"And this is a deal from me," said Mr. Thornton, giving Higgins's hand a good grip. "Now mind, you come sharp to your time," continued he, resuming the master. "I'll have no laggards at my mill. What fines we have, we keep pretty sharply. And the first time I catch you making mischief, off you go. So now you know where you are."

"Yo' spoke of me wisdom this morning. I reckon I

132

may bring it wi' me; or would yo' rayther have me 'bout my brains!"

"'Bout your brains if you use them for meddling with my business; with your brains if you can keep to your own."

"I shall need a deal o' brains to settle where my business ends and yo'rs begins."

"Your business has not begun yet, and mine stands still for me. So good afternoon."

And in fact whenever Mrs. Gaskell is among the lives of people—and the half-starving Darkshire workers with their deathbeds, their drunks and their touch of fantastic Methodism are a different human species from the ladies of Cranford— she has a true eye and ear.

In all her work from *Cranford* onwards, Mrs. Gaskell is the neat social historian. First of all she is the historian of the impecunious genteel, then her net is thrown wider until, in *Wives and Daughters*, it catches a whole society from the aristocracy and the squirearchy down to the professions and trades. "Why", Molly Gibson, the doctor's daughter, asks Lady Harriet, "why do you speak of my class as if we were a strange kind of animal instead of human beings?" That question Mrs. Gaskell put to all classes. In her own way, Mrs. Gaskell was a Lady Harriet, an animal collector. She never gets speech wrong, from dialect to drawl. So that when she came to social strife in *North and South*—and it may be remembered that Dickens published her immediately after *Hard Times* —she had the practice of faithful record. The streets and, again, the manners of the streets in that northern town are done with the fidelity of a Dutch painting, though never overdone. She observes not only particular looks and phrases, but the general look, the drift of the common gossip. She contrasts the brutality of the mill atmosphere with the super-stition of Margaret's beloved Hampshire village. With the reproachfulness of the good but detached Unitarian lady, she notes how both places go blindly on in the pursuit of their own magic. The chapters of discussion are not good, they stick out like lectures, simply because Mr. Hale is in them and Mr. Hale is a failure. (He is the inevitably Victorian tribute to the tedious pathos of self-pity.) But there is one passage of discussion which strikes the eye nowadays because of its curious modern echo. Thornton is answering the liberal intellectual Platonist from Oxford:

> "Remember we are of a different race from the Greeks. . . . I belong to Teutonic blood; it is little mingled in this part of England to what it is in others; we retain much of their language; we retain more of their spirit; we do not look upon life as a time of enjoyment, but as a time for action and exertion."

(He would certainly get that in marrying Mildred.) The don cuts him short when Thornton declares for tribal independence:

> "In short you would like the Heptarchy back again. You are regular worshippers of Thor."

Rosenberg in Yorkshire! Is it an inevitable phase in the development of new communities which are feeling their strength? The discussion ends in the air, indeed it is cut short by a more familiar Mrs. Gaskell who has the art of introducing a distrait remark which will also indicate a fresh touch to the development of a situation. Her sister writes from Corfu (Margaret suddenly interjects), that calico is cheaper and better there! Just a small, trite remark apropos of nothing and yet, what has the author done? She has shown that Margaret is beginning to get interested in the vulgar textile trade—a sign favourable for Mr. Thornton—and that before long Mr. Thornton will have to keep his eye on foreign competition. It would be foolish to make much of a point of such a detail, but Mrs. Gaskell's work was built out of thousands of small, light, truthful touches. The parish visitor sees what is in a room, though she may not grasp the forces that have made that room what it is. In the long domestic gossip of that visit, Mrs. Gaskell is one of the quickest pairs of eyes, one of the frankest tongues.

THE PROXIMITY OF WINE

THE desire for settlement comes with peculiar force to
stockbrokers; but the wish of Mr. Crotchet, the retired
City man of Weybridge, is common to us all:

"The sentimental against the rational," said Mr. Crotchet,
"the intuitive against the inductive, the ornamental against
the useful, the intense against the tranquil, the romantic
against the classical: these are the great and interesting
controversies which I should like, before I die, to see satis-
factorily settled."

Even those of us who have not the disputacious, metaphysical
Scottish blood which Peacock had slyly infused into the veins
of Mr. Crotchet, may join in his unhopeful sigh. What is
the good of inviting intellectuals down for the week end unless
they settle matters like these once and for all? Alas, the habit
of the intellectual is to be unsettling and in both senses of the
word. There is a chronic Mr. Firedamp in every *posse* of the
brainy; even when final order seems to have been achieved,
there is always one bat left in the belfries:

"There is another great question," said Mr. Firedamp,
"greater than those, seeing that it is necessary to be alive
in order to settle any question and this is the question of
water against human woe. Wherever there is water, there
is *malaria*, and wherever there is malaria there are the
elements of death. The great object of a wise man should
be to live on a gravelly hill, without so much as a duckpond
within 10 miles of him, eschewing cisterns and water
butts. . . ."

Dr. Folliott, a Tory and a practical man, had at any rate,

the answer in his cellar. "The proximity of wine", he said, was of more importance "than the longinquity of water." After sufficient Burgundy the endless and cantankerous algebra of life appears lucid and limited. Wine has the triple merit of enriching the vocabulary, cheering the heart, and narrowing the mind, and the sooner one cuts the cackle of the intellectuals with some good food and drink the sooner comes peace on earth.

The food and drink question is fundamental in Peacock. On Samuel Butler's theory that all Radicals have bad digestions, it is clear that from the wine and food test Peacock comes out true-blue Tory. There is no stab of that sublimated belly-ache which drives the rest of us into progressive politics. Of course we know that Peacock called himself a Liberal and wrote for the Liberal reviews; but the enemies of the Utili-tarians considered him a joke and Hazlitt teased him for "warbling" on the wrong side of the fence.

The game Peacock played was a dangerous one, and in a man less original and gifted it would have been disastrous. Peacock's virtue was that he had no political opinions in a very political age; or rather, that he had all the opinions, as a dog has fleas in order to keep his mind off being a dog. Peacock's mind kept open house and ruled the table; too often that leads, in literary circles, to banging the table. One can see this in the Rev. Dr. Folliott. A great character, perhaps the greatest of the Peacock characters, but how close the guzzling clergyman comes to being one of those vinous boors, one of those bottled, no-nonsense dogmatists who tyrannise the table and bully the world of letters with comic bluster about their common sense:

MR. MACQUEDY. Then, sir, I presume you set no value on the right principles of rent, profit, wages and currency.

REVD. DR. FOLLIOTT. My principles, sir, in these things are to take as much as I can get and to pay no more than I can help. These are everyman's principles, whether they be the right principles or no. There, sir, is political economy in a nutshell.

There is too great a finality in the well-fed; and though Dr. Folliott redresses a balance and is a brilliant and mature device for winding the theorists back to the earth—very necessary in the novel of ideas—one's mind does wander to "poor Mrs. Folliott" who, having combed her husband's wig, is firmly left at home. One remembers other poor Mrs. Folliotts pecking a timid and hen-like way behind their boozy, commonsensical cockalorums. And while we have still got political economy in a nutshell it is interesting to note how strong a respect for money is ingrained in the crackling, phlegmatic temper of our satirical writers. It is strong in Iago, it is strong in Swift (the Drapier letters), Shaw is an enthusiastic accountant and Peacock's principles regarding paper money amount to mania. On that subject he was a Firedamp. We may imagine his reactions when, having invited Shelley to live in Marlow, he heard that the poet was giving away his clothes and his money to the indigent inhabitants. It is always surprising when poetic justice is benevolent, and most critics have gasped with incredulous satisfaction at Peacock's luck in hooking a job worth £2,000 a year or more out of the East India Company; what is significant and even more poetically fitting is that Peacock was a success at the job. He it was who organised the building and dispatch of the flat-bottomed gunboats used by the company in the East. There blossomed the Utilitarian. One doubts whether Wordsworth was as efficient at the Excise.

The life of Peacock covers a period of enormous differences. One of Peacock's modern critics, Mr. John Mair, has pointed out how fantastic is the range of his life.

He lived through the French Revolution and the Great Exhibition; he could have read his first books to Nelson and his last to Bernard Shaw [who would not have understood it], Dr. Johnson died a year before his birth and Yeats was born a year before his death. He both preceded and survived Byron, Shelley, Keats and Macaulay; he was contemporary with Rowlandson and with Landseer.

For a satirical mind this was the perfect feast; history at its most conflicting and indigestible. For a temperament liable to be infected by all schools of thought in turn and unable to resist cocking snooks at them, here was wealth. Peacock dined off his disabilities and one can almost hear his unholy highbrow cackle when he finds himself not only pre-dating but surviving his victims. Some annoyance has been felt because he became a kind of reactionary by default; you ought not to pull the leg of your own party. But could there have been a more delightful occupation for one whose baptismal water had a drop of the acid of perversity in it? A Grub Street hack in his time, and one who (according to Hazlitt anyway) overpraised as wildly as any of our commercial reviewers, he sneers at the puffs of Grubb Street. A hater of Scotsmen, he was a theoretical Scotsman for, as Professor Saintsbury discovered, Peacock was baptised at the Scottish kirk. He scarifies Miss Philomel Poppyseed for saying true love is impossible on less than £1,000 a year but is as acute about the marriage settlements of his own characters as Jane Austen herself. Everywhere the satirist is reacting against his own wishes and disappointments. There is little doubt that an erratic education fostered his originality as it also failed to provide some strong stamp which would have made up his mind; there would have been no Peacock if he had gone to the University. But those sneers at the University which always crop up in his books are prolonged; and when the debates between the deteriorationists, the progressives, the transcendentalists and rational economists bore us, we cannot reject the suspicion that Peacock spent a good deal of his literary life training to be an undergraduate.

If Peacock's mind was not made up, if he snapped at his

opponents and his friends, it would be a mistake to think of him as a complete *farceur*. When the effervescence has died down there is a deposit of belief which is not party belief but is rather his century's habit of mind. The eighteenth century had formed him; he belonged to that middleman and professional class which did not share—at least, did not directly share—in the rewards of the industrial revolution. When Mr. Escot speaks against the mills in *Headlong Hall*, he is not putting a party view; he is pleading like a merchant philosopher for the content of living in a world that was violently altering its form in the optimistic delusion that the content would look after itself. If Mr. Peacock-Escot is a reactionary, then one can only reply that it is the rôle of reactionaries, once they have given up obstruction, to remind us that the Sabbath was made for man. Their function is to preserve amenities and that private humanity which revolutionaries care for so little. Here is Mr. Escot with his everything-is-as-bad-as-it-can-be-in-the-worst-of-possible-worlds:

> You present to me a complicated picture of artificial life, and require me to admire it. Seas covered with vessels; every one of which contains two or three tyrants, and from fifty to a thousand slaves, ignorant, gross, perverted and active only in mischief. Ports resounding with life: in other words with noise and drunkenness, the mingled din of avarice, intemperance and prostitution. Profound researches, scientific inventions: to what end? To contract the sum of human wants? to teach the art of living on a little? to disseminate independence, liberty and health? No; to multiply factitious desires, to stimulate depraved appetites, to invent irrational wants, to heap up incense on the shrine of luxury, and accumulate expedients of selfish and ruinous profusion.

He goes on to a description of children in the cotton mills, a true piece of Dickensian phantasmagoria—"observe their pale and ghastly features, more ghastly in that baleful and malignant light and tell me if you do not fancy yourself on the threshold of Virgil's Hell. . . ." Did that passage have any effect on the more ruthless of Peacock's readers? One doubts it. The voice of the Age of Reason was reactionary and decadent from the point of view of the nineteenth-century liberals, and most of us were born into the nineteenth century's belief that a period is decadent which has arrived at the civilised stillness of detached self-criticism. Peacock said the wise thing in the wrong way, i.e. the detached way. It was the attached people, more vulgar, more sentimental, more theatrically subject to the illusions of the new period, who could and did attack child labour and the mills with some effect.

For a man as mercurial and unseizable as Peacock was, what really counted was the farce. Detached, isolated, hiding caution behind a fantasticating brain, silent about the private urges of his heart, unimaginative, timid of "acrimonious dispute" (as the scathing so often are), he enjoyed the irresponsibilities of an intellect which cannot define its responsibilities. His cruelty to his victims is merely the brain's. There he can display an extravagance which elsewhere a prudent nature denies him. His satire was not resented, as far as one knows, by the victims. Shelley laughed at Scythrop in *Nightmare Abbey*. No doubt Shelley's own irresponsibility responded to Peacock's distorted picture of him torn between Harriet and Mary Godwin, "like a shuttlecock between two battledores, changing its direction as rapidly as the oscillations of a pendulum receiving many a hard knock on the cork"—the cork!—"of a sensitive heart and flying from point to point in the feathers of a super-sublimated head".

As they come fragmentarily into focus, the Peacock novels have the farcical dream-atmosphere of the sur-realists' dreams. Their slapstick and their unexpected transitions, their burlesque discussions, and their fancy lead through *Alice in Wonderland* to the present. It is amusing to find present parallels for the deteriorationist and the rational economist. Peacock chose permanent types; but without the knock-about and the romance, that amusement would soon become bookish and musty. Scythrop concealing his lady in the tower and lying about the movable bookcase, Mr. Toobad jumping out of the window at the sight of the "ghost" and being fished out of the moat by the dreary scientists who are down there with their nets fishing for mermaids, Squire Headlong's experiments with explosives, Dr. Folliott's adventures with the highwaymen—this picaresque horseplay is the true stuff of the English comic tradition from Sterne and Fielding, a new gloss on the doings of the Pickwick Club. And Peacock can alternate the perfunctory with the heroic manner, which our tradition especially requires. Gradually, as he perfected his genre, progressing from the Hall to the Abbey, from the Abbey to the Castle, Peacock balanced his extremes. Romantic love plays its part, not the wild meadowy stuff of course, but a romance which secretes an artificial sweetness, the *faux naturel* of the eighteenth century, which at once suggests the formal and untutored. In this heady world the women alone—if one excepts the highbrow Poppyseed and the awful Mrs. Glowry—have the sense and sensibility. Peacock cuts short the sighs; marriages are arranged, not made in Heaven, dowries are not forgotten; but what a delightful convention (the India clerk reminds us) marriage is.

One might expect more broadness in so keen a reader of Rabelais, but Peacock (unless my memory is bad or my ear for *double entendre* dull) appears to share the primness of Dr. Folliott, a primness one often finds among the drinkers. There is only one smoke-room remark in *Crotchet Castle*—and a very good one it is. It occurs after the cook has set her room on fire when she has fallen asleep over a treatise on hydrostatics in cookery:

LORD BOSSNOWL.   But, sir, by the bye, how came your
footman to be going into your cook's room?   It was very
providential, to be sure but . . .

REVD. DR. FOLLIOTT.   Sir, as good came of it, I shut my
eyes and ask no questions.   I suppose he was going to
study hydrostatics and he found himself under the necessity
of practising hydraulics.

I suppose it should be argued that Dr. Folliott's anger about
the exhibition of an undraped female figure on the stockbroker's
mantelpiece was grounded less in the prudery of the bibulous
than in the general Peacockian dislike of popular education.
He was against putting ideas into his footman's head.   An act
of benevolence, for no one knew so well as Peacock how
funny a man with an idea in his head can be.

AN ANATOMY OF GREATNESS

THERE are two books which are the perfect medicine for the present time: Voltaire's *Candide* and Fielding's *Jonathan Wild*. They deal with our kind of news but with this advantage over contemporary literature: the news is already absorbed, assumed and digested. We see our situation at a manageable remove. This is an important consolation and, on the whole, *Jonathan Wild* is the more specific because the narrower and more trenchant book. Who, if not ourselves, are the victims of what are called "Great Men"? Who can better jump to the hint that the prig or cut-purse of Newgate and the swashbuckler of Berchtesgaden are the same kind of man and that Cæsar and Alexander were morally indistinguishable from the gang leaders, sharpers, murderers, pickpockets from whom Mr. Justice Fielding, in later years, was to free the City of London? Europe has been in the hands of megalomaniacs for two decades. Tyranny abroad, corruption at home—that recurrent theme of the eighteenth-century satirists who were confronted by absolute monarchy and the hunt for places—is our own. Who are we but the good—with a small middle-class "g"—and who are "they" but the self-elected "leaders" and "the Great"? And *Jonathan Wild* has the attraction of a great *tour de force* which does not shatter us because it remains, for all its realism, on the intellectual plane. Where Swift, in contempt, sweeps us out of the very stables; where Voltaire advises us not to look beyond our allotments upon the wilderness humanity has left everywhere on a once festive earth, Fielding is ruthless only to the brain. Our heads are scalped by him but soul and body are left alive. He is arbitrary but not destructive. His argument that there is an incompatibility between greatness and goodness is an impossible one, but of the eighteenth century's three scourgers of mankind he is the least egotistical and the most moral. He has not destroyed the world; he has merely turned it upside down as a polished dramatist will force a play out of a paradox:

"... contradicting the obsolete doctrines of a Set of Simple Fellows called, in Derision, Sages or Philosophers, who have endeavoured as much as possible to confound the Ideas of Greatness and Goodness, whereas no two Things can possibly be more distinct from each other. For Greatness consists in bringing all Manner of Mischief on Mankind, and Goodness in removing it from them."

Jonathan Wild is a paradox sustained with, perhaps the strain, but above all, with the decisiveness, flexibility and exhilaration of a scorching trumpet call which does not falter for one moment and even dares very decorative and difficult variations on the way to its assured conclusion. When we first read satire we are aware of reading against the whole current of our beliefs and wishes, and until we have learned that satire is anger laughing at its own futility, we find ourselves protesting and arguing silently against the author. This we do less, I think, in reading *Jonathan Wild* than with *Candide* or *Gulliver*. If there is any exhaustion in *Jonathan Wild* it does not come from the tussle of our morality with his. There is no moral weariness. If we tire it is because of the intellectual effort of reversing the words "great" and "good" as the eye goes over the page. Otherwise it is a young man's book, very vain of its assumptions and driven on with masterly nonchalance.

To the rigidity of his idea Fielding brought not only the liveliness of picaresque literature but, more important, his experience as a playwright. Of its nature satire deals in types and artifices and needs the schooling of the dramatist, who can sweep a scene off the moment the point is made and who can keep his nimble fingers on a complicated plot. Being concerned with types, satire is in continual need of intrigue and movement; it needs tricks up the sleeve and expertness in surprise. We are distracted in *Jonathan Wild* between pleasure in his political references (the pointed one on the quarrels between the gangsters about the style of their hats for example, which Wild settles with the genius of a dictator), and the dexterity of the author. "Great men are lonely": one of the best scenes in the book, one fit to stand beside Wild's wonderful quarrel with his wife Tishy when he calls her a bitch, is the superb comedy of Wild's soliloquy in the boat. Put adrift in an open boat by the Captain who has rescued Heartfree's wife from Wild's attempt at rape, Wild has his "black Friday" and muses on the loneliness of "the Great", their fear of death and their unhappiness. Since death is inevitable, Wild cries, why not die now? A man of action, for ever acting to an audience if only an imaginary one, he staggers us by at once throwing himself into the sea. Were we wrong? Was he courageous after all? We knew that a crook lives on gestures, that a show of toughness is all—but were we misreading him? Down comes the curtain, the chapter ends. Its dramatic effect is enormous, quite beyond the reach of the picaresque novelists who depend on the convolutions of intrigue alone. Among the satirists, only Voltaire, another writer for the stage, was capable of Fielding's scene; Swift was always willing to let a situation ease off into ironical discussion. And then, up goes Fielding's curtain again: Wild does not die. He is saved. He is in a boat once more. Saved by one of those disillusioning miracles of fiction? Not at all. He is back in his own boat. *He swam back to it.* Philosophy had told him to die, but Nature, whom he knew had designed him to be Great, told him not to be such a fool. That is a masterstroke.

146

Such cross-ruffing is the heart of farce and of the ordinary literature of roguery.   But as Wild picks the pockets of his accomplices, double-crosses the card-sharping Count, swindles and is swindled in turn, each act shows a further aspect of his character and is a new chapter in the anatomy of Greatness. It has been said that Fielding's common sense and his low opinion that human beings were moved chiefly by self-interest, restricted his imagination.   This may be so, though the greater restriction was to his sensibility.   In the light of our present painful knowledge of Great Men of action we are not likely to think the portrait of Wild unimaginative simply because Fielding takes an unpoetical view.   There is the episode of the jewels.   The Count who, with Wild, has swindled Heart-free over the casket of jewels, has double-crossed his partner by substituting paste for the stolen treasure.   Worse still, Tishy whom Wild intends to seduce by the gift of the casket, has worked in a pawnbroker's and knows paste when she sees it. Wild is left to another soliloquy, to the sadness of Berchtesgaden or neo-Imperial Rome.   "They" are always sad:

> How vain is human Greatness! . . .   How unhappy is the state of Priggism!   How impossible for Human Prudence to foresee and guard against each circumvention! . . .   In this a Prig is more unhappy than any other: a cautious man may in a crowd, preserve his own Pockets by keeping his hands in them; but while he employs his Hands in another's pockets, how shall he be able to defend his own?   Where is his Greatness?   I answer in his Mind; 'Tis the inward Glory, the secret Consciousness of doing great and wonderful Actions, which can alone support the truly Great Man, whether he be a Conqueror, a Tyrant, a Minister or a Prig. These must bear him up against the private Curse and public Imprecation, and while he is hated and detested by all Mankind, must make him inwardly satisfied with himself. For what but some such inward satisfaction as this could inspire Men possessed of Wealth, of Power, of every human

Blessing, which Pride, Luxury, or Avarice could desire, to forsake their Homes, abandon Ease and Repose, and, at the Expense of Riches, Pleasures, at the Price of Labour and Hardship, and at the Hazard of all that Fortune hath liberally given them could send them at the Head of a Multitude of *Prigs* called an Army, to molest their Neighbours, to introduce Rape, Rapine, Bloodshed and every kind of Misery on their own Species? What but some such glorious Appetite of Mind. . . .

Intoxicating stuff. The eighteenth century's attack on absolutism, its cry of Liberty, its plea for the rational, the measured, and even the conventional culminated—in what? Napoleon. And then democracy. It is painful to listen to the flying Prigs, to democracy's *Jonathan Wild*. Was the moral view of human nature mistaken? Is the Absolute People as destructive as the Absolute King? Is the evil not in the individual, but in society? We rally to the eighteenth-century cry of "Liberty"; it is infectious, hotter indeed than it sounds today. We reflect that those good, settled, educated, middle-class men of the time of Queen Anne, owed their emancipation to a Tyrant who burned half Ireland, killed his King and went in private hysterical dread of the devil. Under that smooth prose, under that perfect deploying of abstractions, the men of the eighteenth century seem always to be hiding a number of frightening things that are neither smooth nor perfect. There is the madness of Swift, there is the torment of Wesley. Or was Fielding imagining the paradise of the anarchists where our natural goodness enables us to dispense with leaders? Sitting under the wings of the flying Prigs, we observe the common, indeed the commonplace, non-combatant man, behaving with a greatness which appears to require no leader but merely the prompting of sober and decent instincts.

Of course if the Great are wicked, the good are fools. Look at the Heartfrees! What a couple! But here again if you have made your head ache over Fielding's impossible theme, it is cured at once by the felicities to which the Heartfrees drive Fielding's invention. The letters which Heartfree gets from his impecunious or disingenuous debtors are a perfect collection; and Mrs. Heartfree's sea adventures in which there is hardly a moment between Holland and Africa when she is not on the point of losing her honour, are not so much padding but give a touch of spirit to her shopkeeping virtues and also serve the purpose of satirising the literature of travel. It is hard on Mrs. Heartfree; perhaps Fielding was insensitive. Without that insensibility we should have missed the adventure with the monster who was "as large as Windsor Castle", an episode which reminds us that the spirit of the 9 o'clock news was already born in the seventeen-hundreds:

> I take it to be the strangest Instance of that Intrepidity, so justly remarked in our Seamen, which can be found on Record. In a Wood then, one of our Mucketeers coming up to the Beast, as he lay on the Ground and with his Mouth wide open, marched directly down his Throat.

He had gone down to shoot the Monster in the heart. And we should have missed another entrancing sight. Mrs. Heartfree perceived a fire in the desert and thought at first she was approaching human habitation.

> . . . but on nearer Approach, we perceived a very Beautiful Bird just expiring in the Flames. This was none other than the celebrated Phœnix.

The sailors threw it back into the Fire so that it "might follow its own Method of propagating its Species".

Yes, the Heartfrees would have a lot to talk about afterwards. There is a charm in the artlessness of Mrs. Heartfree, if Heartfree is a bit of a stodge; one can understand why she introduced just a shade of suspense in the account of how she always managed to save her virtue at the last minute.

THE DEAN

THE world would be poor without the antics of clergymen. The Dean, for example, wished he was a horse. A very Irish wish which a solid Englishwoman very properly came down on; Lady Mary Wortley Montagu was one of the few hostile critics of *Gulliver*:

> Great eloquence have (the authors) employed to prove themselves beasts and show such a veneration for horses, that, since the Essex Quaker nobody has appeared so passionately devoted to that species; and to say truth they talk of a stable with so much warmth and affection I cannot help suspecting some very powerful motive at the bottom of it.

It *was* odd that a man as clean as the Dean should find solace among the mangers; and there is a stable tip for psychoanalysts here. The function which he loathed in Celia and could never stop mentioning, had become unnoticeable at last. Shades of the Freudian Cloacina imprison the growing boy, but are guiltlessly charmed away when, pail and shovel in hand, we make our first, easy, hopeful acquaintance with the fragrant Houhynhms.

Dr. Johnson was also hostile. *Gulliver* was written "in defiance of truth and regularity". Yet the Dean and the Doctor had much in common. They were both sensible men in a century devoted to the flightiness of Reason. What annoyed the Doctor was what enchanted the public; the *madness* of *Gulliver*. Very irregular. We see now that the Augustan prose was a madman's mask and that the age of Reason was also the age of witchcraft, hauntings, corruption and the first Gothic folly. History has confirmed Dr. Johnson's judgment first by numbing the satire—for who can be bothered to look up the digs at Walpole, Newton and the rest?—and by giving the book a totally different immortality. It is not an accident· that *Gulliver* has become a child's book; only a child could be so destructive, so irresponsible and so cruel. Only a child has the animal's eye; only a child, or the mad clergyman, can manage that unhuman process of disassociation which is the beginning of all satire from Aristophanes onwards; only children (or the mad) have that monstrous and infantile egotism which assumes everything is meaningless and that, like children, we run the world on unenlightened self-interest like a wagon-load of monkeys. What a relief it is that the Dean's style is as lucid and plain as common water: it runs like water off a duck's back. If *Gulliver* had been written in the coloured prose of the Bible, bulging with the prophetic attitudinisings of the Jews, the book might have caused a revolution—there is some very revolutionary stuff in Lilliput—but a moderate church Tory like the Dean had no intention of doing that. There must have been satisfaction in reminding a Queen in the rational century that under her petticoat she was a Yahoo and savage satisfaction in knowing she liked the idea. In this she was a sensible woman; she had, like the rest of us, been charmed back to the minute and monstrous remembrances of childhood, she had been captivated by the plain, good and homely figure of Gulliver himself. She picked out the topical bits and when the Dean waded into his generalities about human nature, her eyes no doubt wandered off that almost too easy page and examined her finger-nails.

But there was a part of *Gulliver* which nobody liked or which most people thought inferior. Laputa missed the mark. Why? It was topical enough. The skit on science was a good shot at the young Royal Society and the wave of projects which obsessed the times. The highbrow is always fair game. Visually and· satirically Laputa is the most delightful of the episodes. The magic island floats crystalline in the air, rising and falling to the whim of its ruler, and its absent-minded philosophers are only tickled into awareness by a fly-whisk. Laputa is the rationalist's daydream. Here is the unearthly paradise, an hydraulic and attainable heaven. True, the philosophers were fools and the scientists, with their attempts to get sunshine out of cucumbers, cloth from spiders, food from dirt and panic from astronomy, were ridiculous. The knowledge machine was grotesque. But what was the matter with the men of Newton's time that they could not appreciate Laputa? The age of Reason enjoyed the infantile, the animal and irrational in *Gulliver*; it rejected the satire on knowledge.

The only answer can be that the Augustans had not had enough of science, to know it was worth satirising. The Dean was before his time; and the world would have to wait a hundred and fifty years for *Bouvard and Pécuchet* to continue the unpopular game—the origins of *Bouvard* and *Gulliver* are, incidentally, identical and both Flaubert and Swift spent ten years on and off writing the books—and among ourselves, we have only Aldous Huxley's crib of Laputa, *Brave New World*. Yet Laputa is the only part of *Gulliver* which has not been eclipsed by subsequent writing. Voltaire, Wells, Verne—to take names at random—have all taken the freshness off Swift's idea; and what the Utopians have left out has been surpassed by science itself. The sinister functionalism of the termites, the pedestrian mysticism of the bee, the ribald melodramas of the aquarium and the Grand Guignol of the insect house, have all defeated human life and literature as material for the political satirist. These things have put the date on Lilliput, but Laputa is untouched. It stands among us, miraculously contemporary.

It is the sur-realist island. At least Laputa is to Lilliput what Alice in Wonderland is to sur-realism. The sportively clinical and sinister, succeed to the human and extraordinary.

One cannot love Laputa as one loves Lilliput, but one *recognises* Laputa. It is the clinic we have come to live in. It is the world of irresponsible intellect and irresponsible science which prepared the way for the present war. We enter at once into our inhumanity, into that glittering laboratory which is really a butcher's shop. What science does not dissect, it blows to pieces. The Dean, safe at the beginning of the period, did not foresee this—though he does note that, to crush rebellion, the King was in the habit of letting the island down bodily from the sky on the rebellious inhabitants.

We are also in the world of the cubist painters. The rhomboid joints, the triangular legs of mutton come out of Wyndham Lewis—has he illustrated Laputa?—those mathematicians take us to our Bertrand Russells. Among the astronomers, with their weakness for judicial astrology, does one not detect the philosophical speculations of Jeans and Eddington? Pure thought, moreover, led to a laxity of morals, for husbands devoted to the higher intellectual life were inclined either to be short-sighted or absent-minded, and the wives in Laputa found it necessary and simple to descend to coarser but more attentive lovers on the mainland below. In search perhaps of Gerald Heard's new mutation, the speculative despised sex or forgot about it; or having read their *Ends and Means*, thought of giving sex up. Yes, Laputa, the island of the non-attached, is topical.

Like all satirists, the Dean was, nevertheless, in a vulnerable position. By temperament and in style he is one of the earliest scientific writers in modern literature. He delights, with a genuine anticipation of scientific method, in those measurements of hoofs, heads and fingers, the calculated quantities of food, the inevitable observation on his bladder. One might be reading Malinowski or Dr. Zuckermann. Yet when one puts the book down it is to realise that there is one more country in the story which is the counterblast to Laputa, Lilliput and the whole list. This is Gulliver himself. The world is mad, grotesque, a misanthropic Irishman's self-destructive fantasy; but Gulliver is not. Gulliver is sane. He is good, homely, friendly and decent. How he keeps himself to himself in his extraordinary adventures! No love affairs; Mrs. Gulliver and family are waiting at home. Unlike the philosophers, he is not a cuckold. One is sure he isn't.

"I have ever hated all nations, professions and communities," the Dean wrote to Pope; "and all my love is towards individuals; for instance I hate the tribe of lawyers, but I love Councillor Such a One and Judge Such a One; principally I hate and detest that animal called man, although I heartily love John, Peter, Thomas and so forth."

A religious mind, even one as moderate in its religion as Swift's, must, in the end, be indifferent to material welfare, progress and hopes. Gulliver is simply John, Peter or Thomas, the ordinary sensible man and he stands alone against the mad laboratories of the floating island. Gulliver could not know that people would one day make a knowledge machine or invent sunshine substitutes (but not out of cucumbers), but he does know that it is folly to let the world be run by these people. They will turn it (as the visit to Lagado showed, or, shall we say, to a blitzed town) into a wilderness. The world, the mad Dean says in the figure of Gulliver, must be run by John, Peter, Thomas, the sensible man.

THE END OF THE GAEL

THE return of Synge from Paris to Ireland is a dramatic moment in Anglo-Irish literature. In significance that journey is equalled only by the one made in the other direction by Joyce when he broke with Dublin for ever and went angrily to the Continent. The thing which fired Synge seemed to Joyce to be tarnished by the vulgarity of Edwardian Dublin. Unhappily the dates do not quite fit, but nevertheless one has a picture of those two figures, most self-contained and priest-like in their attitude to literature, passing each other without signals of recognition on their opposite journeys across the Irish Sea. Each is going to what the other has left: Joyce is on his way to become something like the Irish pedant and æsthete abroad, moving to that diletantism which always seems to catch the Irishman in exile, turning him into a kind of cold Tara brooch in the shirt-front of Western European culture; and Synge is on the way back to rub off some of the polish and to refertilise an imagination which culture had sterilised. Such migrations, exile and return, are a master rhythm in Irish life. And yet, when one thinks about these journeys in connection with the work of Synge and Joyce, their destinations are not effectively so different after all. Both writers are sedulous linguists and lovers of a phrase who sport like dolphins in the riotous oceans of an English language which has something of the fabulous air of a foreign tongue for them. In the beginning was the word—if that is not the subject of their work, it is the exciting principle. There would even be no difficulty in citing parallel passages. I have no copy of *Ulysses* or *Finnegan* to hand at the moment, but sentences from *The Playboy* like Christy's

"Ah, you'll have a gallous jaunt, I'm saying, coaching
out through limbo with my father's ghost",

or,

"And I must go back into my torment is it, or run off
like a vagabond straying through the unions with the dust
of August making mudstains in the gullet of my throat;
or the winds of March blowing on me till I'd take an oath
I felt them making whistles of my ribs within",

are three parts on the way to *Anna Livia*.   And this passion
for the bamboozling and baroque of rhetoric leaves both Synge
and Joyce with a common emotion: an exhausted feeling of
the evanescence of outward things, which is philosophical in
Synge and, in Joyce, the very description of human conscious-
ness.   The sense of a drunken interpenetration of myth or
legend (or should we call it imagination and the inner life)
with outer reality is common to them.   Where modern Euro-
peans analysed, Synge and Joyce, heirs of an earlier culture,
substituted metaphor and image.   Again and again, in almost
any page you turn to in Joyce and Synge, the tragedy or comedy
of life is felt to be the tragedy or comedy of memory and the
imagination.   It is their imagination which transforms Christy,
Pegeen, Deirdre, and Nora in *The Shadow of the Glen*; but
when, "the fine talk they have on them" is done, they are
aware that time is writing on like a ledger clerk, that the
beautiful girls will become old hags like the Widow Quin or
Mrs. Bloom grunting among her memories on the chamber-pot.
Time dissolves the lonely legendary mind of man, killing the
spells of the heart, draining the eloquence of the body—that
seems to be not only the subject of Synge's *Deirdre* and all his
plays, but the fundamental subject of Anglo-Irish literature.

Reading Synge again one feels all the old excitement of his
genius.   Nothing has faded.   He reads as well as an Eliza-
bethan.   In his short creative period all Synge's qualities were

brought to a high pitch of intensity and richness and his work stands inviolable in a world apart. It is unaffected by the passing of the fashion for peasant drama, for behind the peasant addict with his ear to the chink in the wall is the intellect of the European tradition, something of Jonson's grain and gusto. Synge was a master who came to his material at what is perhaps the ripest moment for an artist—the brink of decadence. The Gaelic world was sinking like a ship; and there was an enlightened desperation in the way the Anglo-Irish caught at that last moment, before their own extinction too. That, anyway, is how it looks now. The preoccupation with the solitude of man, with illusion and with the evanescence of life in Synge and Joyce is one of the signs that the old age of a culture has come, and Synge gives to the death of the Gaelic world the nobility and richness of a ritual. It is not, as in the Aran journal, a ritual of sparse sad words, but the festive blaze of life.

It is common in the eulogies of Synge to say that the un-finished *Deirdre of the Sorrows* hints at heights to which Synge's genius might have attained. For me *Deirdre* marks a dubious phase in his development. Even when I allow for the blind spot which English taste has in the matter of legendary or mythological subjects, I cannot help feeling that, in attempting *Deirdre* Synge put himself into a literary straitjacket and went back on the sound opinions he gave in his prefaces to the plays and poems. No doubt anyone who knew Yeats at that time was simply ordered into the Celtic twilight and had to take his dose of it; but one hopes that Synge would have had the sanity to return to the doctrine he set out in the preface to *The Tinker's Wedding*:

> Of the things which nourish the imagination humour is one of the most useful, and it is dangerous to limit or destroy it.

More important:

I have often thought that at the side of the poetic diction which everyone condemns, modern verse contains a great deal of poetic material, using poetry in the same special sense. The poetry of exaltation will be always the highest; but when men lose their poetic feelings for ordinary life and cannot write poetry of ordinary things, their exalted poetry is likely to lose its strength of exaltation, in the way men cease to build beautiful churches when they have lost happiness in building shops.

And more important still, these words from the introduction to his book of poems and translations:

The drama is made serious—in the French sense of the word—not by the degree in which it is taken up with the problems that are serious in themselves, but by the degree in which it gives nourishment, not very easy to define, on which our imaginations live.

So *Riders to the Sea* seems to me genuinely tragic tragedy, but *Deirdre* to be simply poetic material for tragedy where Synge's genius moves stiffly.

Like the Russians in the 'seventies, Synge "returned to the people" when he went to Aran. Unlike the Russians he does not seem to have felt any mystical faith in doing this, and knew quite well that the heroic, primitive life of the West was doomed. There is always the sensation in Synge's work of being one of the last men on earth, the survivor of a dying family. One feels the loneliness of men and women in a lonely scene, and one is also made to feel the personal, inaccessible loneliness of Synge himself. At the back of the plays there is, for all his insistence on the necessity of joy and feasting in the theatre, a dark and rather *fin de siècle* shadow, and there is more than a hint, in the character of the Playboy, of the art-for-art's-sake artist of the 'nineties who lives only in words and illusions. Joyce's legendary Dublin is, in a sense, the answer to Synge's legendary West. *Ulysses* is an assertion that modern urban man can have his myth and Joyce's "ordinary men" are the sort of "ordinary men" whom Synge would have found lifeless. Synge was too soon to see the enormous contribution of the American vernacular to popular culture in the towns, and too cut off from the knowledge of urban people to know what resources common urban speech had. Nowadays (and without mistaking courage for the Heroic pattern of living) we can discern the new heroic status of cities in their Æschylean devastation and their curious mass stoicism. Cities seem now to have become greater, in this sense, than individual men.

In one obvious way Synge does belong to an earlier world than ours, and that is in his humour. It is the strong, sculptured, corporeal and baroque humour of knavery, tricks and cunning. We have almost entirely lost the literature of roguery, the life of which has been prolonged in Ireland by the tradition of disrespect for foreign law. To his handling of roguery, Synge brought all the subtlety he had learned from Molière. This has, of course, often been said and it stands out a mile in his handling of the dramatist's use of continual contrast, whereby almost every speech creates a new situation or farcically reverses its predecessor. There is no falsity in his farces; one does not feel that the situation is an artificial one. How easily *The Playboy* could have become Aldwych knockabout; and yet how easily Synge makes us accept his preposterous idea, by trying it first upon the main character before our eyes. The texture of his drama is a continuous interweaving of challenge and riposte, a continuous changing of the threads in a single motif; so that we are involved in far more than a mere anecdote which has a jerk of astonishment in the beginning and a sting in the tail at the end. At the height of farce we may instantly, by a quick shift of focus, be faced by that sense of the evanescence of life which is Synge's especially, or we may be jogged by the sharp elbow of mortality.

And as a piece of music will start on two or three plain notes before its theme is given a head, so these plays start in the simple household accents and come with the same domesticity to their end. The old man having got rid of his wife, changes his tone and calls for the drink, the tinkers escape from the curse of the priest to their old life on the roads, Pegeen is left to clear up at the inn, the blind whom the saint has healed go back to their blindness. All are ordinary people once more, leaving us (as the comic genius does) to eye each other with new, unholy expectation, warming us with the love of human antics, fattening our thin wits, so that like Sir Mammon in *The Alchemist* we cry out as we put the book down, "Oh, my voluptuous mind!"

THE STEEPLE HOUSE SPIRES

O NE hesitates, since Freud, to admit to a strong personal
feeling for church steeples, and yet who does not respond
to the ring and vividness of that phrase which occurs again and
again in George Fox's *Journal* and which puts the man and
his book a key higher than the common chord of living:

> As I was walking in a close with several Friends, I
> lifted up my head and espied three steeple house spires and
> they struck at my life?

They do still strike at our lives, though with the stab of
reminiscence rather than of faith, when we see them rising
over the fields and elms of the English countryside. In the
towns—and Fox, on this occasion was speaking of "the bloody
city of Lichfield"—the steeple commands the skyline no longer.
Those words of Fox, more than any others of his, take us back
to the seventeenth century. In the eighteenth century the
steeple must still have denominated the towns to the arriving
traveller, as it continues today to mark our villages, but did
the steeple strike at the eighteenth-century traveller's life?
That is very doubtful. The decisiveness, the militance, the
poignancy have gone out of English religious fervour. After
the seventeenth century what religion has there been in England? There is only the revivalism of Wesley, a fruit of
personal conflict, and Wesley side-tracked a revolution where
the "prophesyings" of the Puritans made one.

That is perhaps too great a simplification; Fox himself was
a poor short-term revolutionary when one compares him with
Cromwell's sectarian soldiers; the mysticism of the Quakers

161

provided, *in their own time*, an alternative to the revolution, such as we see in the gospels of non-resistance, pacifism, non-attachment, etc., etc., today. If we continue that quotation from Fox's *Journal*, we cannot doubt that it contains a revolutionary emotion which is more dynamic than the feeling of Winstanley's peasant communists, for example, who, having taken the land, were content to keep the clergy and the gentry off by singing a song about "conquering with love".

> I asked [Fox goes on] what place that was and they said, Lichfield. Immediately the word of the Lord came to me that thither I must go. . . . I stepped away, and went by my eye over hedge and ditch till I came within a mile of Lichfield, where in a great field, there were shepherds keeping their sheep. I was commanded of the Lord to untie my shoes and put them off.

And then, his feet burning like fire in the winter fields, he walked into the town where:

> the word of the Lord came to me again, to cry "Woe unto the bloody city of Lichfield!" So I went up and down the streets, crying with a loud voice, "Woe to the bloody city of Lichfield!" . . . And no one laid hands on me; but as I went thus crying through the streets, there seemed to me to be a channel of blood running down the streets, and the market place appeared like a pool of blood.

That is authentic and so is the characteristic English reaction: "Alack George," the inhabitants said, "where are thy shoes?" The woe could take care of itself; what bothered the kindly, respectable, practical souls of Lichfield was the condition of George Fox's feet.

There is the attraction of Fox's *Journal* in a few lines. In his writing the personal fanatic cry of the visionary and the words of the homely are blended. The huge Leicestershire shepherd with his loud voice and his curling hair (which a disapproving Puritan lady in Wales tried to snip off with her scissors), with his horn of snuff and his leathern suit, has his feet on the soil, on the roads of the seventeenth-century English wilderness and in the streets of the muddy towns. He has "great openings". He "sees" this and that. The imps and devils are chained to his foot, the "inner light" burns vividly in him and is easily distinguished from the "false light" of other people's "vain imaginings"; but he also knows the price of oats and how to obstruct magistrates. He can put off a pretentious theologian with the truly peasant remark that if the man thinks he is God, does he know if it is going to rain tomorrow? Unlike Bunyan's Christian traveller, Fox is a real man, travelling on real roads. He knows the inns, the houses of friends, the jails. He was worn out on the Welsh hills, mired on the Yorkshire roads and saw the sea from the edge of Lancashire. From the age of twenty he was wandering all over England, from steeple to steeple, meeting the soldiers on the way to the Battle of Worcester, being beaten by the mobs, taken up by the sheriffs, arguing the Scriptures with Papists, Brownites, Independents, Ranters, "rude jangling Baptists", and the "hireling priests". He was in Cumberland:

> Now were great threatenings given forth in Cumberland that if ever I came there again they would take away my life. When I heard it I was drawn to go into Cumberland. . . .

If he feared any danger it was the danger of remaining in one place where long contact with people would blunt the edge of conscience and dull his ear for the word of the Lord. A man of little education, he is no great writer; his jogtrot Puritan prose ambles like his horse and cannot be compared with Bunyan's. But his own obstinate, innocent alarming character bursts through the repetitions. And the rest of his prose is made up of Biblical echoes, the sound of Hebraic incantation common to evangelical writings but in his time not yet mechanised and turned into cant.

A man of visions Fox lacks the introspective intellect. His mind, for all its exaltation, is even commonplace and he has frequently to fall back upon a dramatic muddle of Biblical metaphor when he is trying to describe his moments of darkness. There was a mysterious temptation, for example,

> that all was of nature, and the elements and storm came over me, so that I was in a manner quite clouded with it.

But the mood, whatever it may have been, passed and

> I was come up in spirit through the flaming sword into the paradise of God. All things were new.

Then the Leicestershire shepherd breaks at last into his own voice:

> All the creation gave another smell unto me than before, beyond what words can utter.

The virtues and vices of Quakerism lie in a startling mildness and literalness of mind. The other sects of the period were in ecstasies of expectation or fear; they bore on their shoulders a back-breaking load of hopes of bliss and fears of damnation. The Quakers, those practical children of the Quietists and the non-attached, dissolved the coagulations of dogma and doctrine, and experienced their heaven and their hell in the present moment. They were in Abraham's bosom *now*. One sees the other Puritans fighting their way towards God as if towards an enemy; the Quakers purified themselves and waited for God to speak like a friend in their hearts. Unoppressed by dogma, unfettered by a programme, they were free to go on with their work or their philanthropy while the factions fought. They went on with their business—hence the jealousy of their wealth. Their affinity is, of course, with Santa Teresa, with her "The Lord walks among the pots and pans"—a mysticism so tamed in their case that from the unreason of "the inner light" sprang the necessity of Tolerance, the first break with the exorbitance of the age of revolution, the first glimmer of the age of Reason, as Professor Trevelyan has pointed out in his book on the Stuarts.

But Fox, the founder, belongs to the dynamic age of Quakerism. We see the familiar human dilemma. Fox preached "the inner light" by throwing many into the outer darkness. "Drowned." "Had a miserable end"—how often one meets this comment on the fate of those who opposed him. A butcher put his tongue out at Fox; the tongue swelled up and would not go back. This is not said gloatingly, but with the fervour of fanaticism for its own logic. If a miraculous healing was impermanent, the patient had "disobeyed the Lord". Those who "see" the truth are "tender" or "very tender"; those who reject it are "rude" or "light chaffy men". Accused of witchcraft himself—when he was beaten Fox did not bleed, or bled very little, for there was a curious lack of blood in his huge frame—he is, of course, expert at discerning witchcraft in others. He speaks of seeing several women who were witches working in a field as he passed. One unhappy woman "with an unclean spirit" had to be turned out of a meeting before he would speak. (His dramatic sense was enormous.) A pistol is fired point-blank at him; naturally it does not go off. And then there is the row about refusing to take the oath. One must sympathise with revolutionary authorities when they are faced by revolutionaries even more revolutionary than themselves. For Fox and his fellow quietists, apostles of non-violence, might turn the other cheek to physical violence but they provoked riots with their tongues. They marched into the steeple-houses crying "Peace be unto you" and in the next breath were denouncing the preacher as a "hireling", preaching him down in his own church, and then became indignant when the police or the soldiers had to come in to restore order. And they were even more indignant when asked to swear the oath of allegiance. Mysticism has always been recognised as a disintegrating force in society. The last thing successful revolutionaries can dispense with is loyalty.

It was an age of hatred and hats. One thinks of each century in terms of some article of fashion or clothing. In the nineteenth century the frock-coat symbolises the cult of political respectability; in the eighteenth century the wig is the emblem of political elegance. In the seventeenth century, there is the hat, the hat jammed down implacably on the brow and worn with a vehemence which has been equalled in the last decade of our own time by the feeling for the shirt. When the Quakers refused to raise their hats to their friends in the street, or in the Courts, they were part of that anti-doffing movement to which Puritans in general subscribed as a protest against the long, feathery and sweeping bows of the Cavaliers. Lilbourne, when brought before the Council of State, had refused to remove his hat to people who had "no more legal authority than myself". It took the Quakers, with their obstinacy, their literalness of mind and their simple way of finding a precise moral justification in the Scriptures, to appeal beyond the courts to God. One cannot decide whether they were vexatious or remarkable in that wonderful judicial comedy which George Fox provoked at Launceston. He writes with pain, but surely with a sly peasant smile of private triumph:

> When we were brought into the Court, we stood a pretty while with our hats on, and all was quiet; and I was moved to say, "Peace be among you!" Judge Glynne, a Welchman, the Chief Justice of England, said to the jailer, "What be these you have brought here into the Court?" "Prisoners, my lord," said he. "Why do you not put off your hats?" said the judge to us; we said nothing. "Put off your hats,"

said the judge again. Still we said nothing. Then said the judge, "The Court commands you to put off your hats." Then I spoke and said "Where did ever any magistrate, king or judge from Moses to Daniel, command any to put off their hats, when they came before them in their courts, either amongst the Jews, the people of God, or among the heathen? And if the law of England doth command any such thing, shew me that law either written or printed." Then the judge grew angry and said "I do not carry my law-books on my back. . . . Take him away, prevaricator. I'll ferk him."

Presently the judge cooled down and called the prisoner back:

"Come," said he, "where had they hats from Moses to Daniel? Come, answer me. I have you fast now."

But George Fox knew the scriptures.

"Thou mayest read," he replied, "in the 3rd of Daniel that the three children were cast into the fiery furnace by Nebuchadnezzar's command, with their coats, their hose and their hats on." This plain instance stopped him so that not having anything else to say to the point, he cried again, "Take them away, jailer."

True anarchists, the Quakers would make a Star Chamber matter of a triviality. Yet their history shows them to have been both conservative and opportunist. They accepted Cromwell, they accepted Charles II; they would accept anybody. What they did not accept was the rule of bureaucracy in matters of belief; and it is interesting that neither Cromwell nor Charles persecuted Fox. Cromwell admired "a people he could not buy", Charles was amused and indifferent. The persecution came from the underlings.

In two countries, Scotland and Ireland, the Leicestershire peasant was not at home. In Scotland he came up against pedants; Presbyterianism was an obdurate enemy of the Quakers. In Ireland, for the first time in the *Journal*, there is a suggestion of bewilderment, distaste and even fear; "The earth smelt, me thought, of the corruption of the nation." The smell, as in Lichfield, was of blood. In Lichfield, the blood shed by Diocletian; in Dublin the blood of the Popish massacres. Not, be it noted, of the Cromwellian massacres. In Cork he felt the peeping eyes at the windows; spies were everywhere; a description of him was sent on a hundred miles ahead in the manner of a sinister jungle message. "A grim black fellow"— an evil spirit—appeared to be chained to his foot. He rode in fear of "the Tories"—gangs of disbanded soldiers—and was relieved to escape them. The voyage back to Liverpool was made in a tempest and in the end of the adventure so prosaically recorded, one sees one last sardonic thrust from the corrupt island. Fox was slanderously accused of having taken to drink.

No, Ireland, for all the "tender" people there and the great meetings, was a nightmare. The Leicestershire shepherd was not made for the dark imaginations which bewitched that country. He was English. One sees him, the big man from a dull flat country, a peasant shrewd and, yet, in a massive way, naif; sober yet obstinate; gentle yet immovably blunt; a man who has made his mind up, who has the inordinate pride and yet the inordinate humility of the saints.

ONE OF OUR FOUNDERS

U P to the early nineteenth century who were the Puritan writers of autobiography? The names of Fox, Bunyan, Defoe, Cobbett and Franklin come to mind first of all. Not all wrote their life-story in a single piece, but the character of their writing is intensely autobiographical. They are plain and homely figures; there is no getting away from that, indeed, it is their boast. Sensibility, elegance, urbanity, imagination and culture are not notable in their natures or their work, the name of Franklin excepted. (The case for Bunyan's imagination fails, I think, because his imagination is a borrowed one, the dream of a mind gorged on the writings of the Hebrews.) If the Reformation turned us into a nation of shopkeepers, these are the men who keep the books. And here, I think, we should distinguish in our use of the words "homely" and "plain". The sense of dull worth and stagnation which has accrued to these adjectives, came to them during the nineteenth century, when the domestic hearth was insulated from the world; but in the eighteenth century and earlier, the meaning had more of nature and less of complacency in it. Those times were nearer the dynamic period of Puritanism, times of revolution, colonisation and travel; and the reader must have noticed, with a smile, how little these prophets of the plain, domestic virtues stayed at home. In a man like Fox, the native restlessness of the virtuous Puritan is explicit: he feared to be corrupted if he stayed too long in one place. Bunyan is on the road or in prison and his Christian is on a journey. Defoe is on tour or in the stocks, and his Crusoe comes home only once every so often to beget a child. Cobbett is perpetually on horseback and Franklin is running away from his relations, crossing and recrossing the Atlantic. What a contrast there is between their precept and example! There they are warning us against the way of the world, but who is more in the world than they?

The answer is that whatever else the ideal of Puritanism may have been, its joint aim was always success. Preaching caution, moderation, industry and sobriety to generations of shopkeepers, round whose necks they tie their moral maxims like a sack of bricks, the great Puritan exemplars pursue not the same course, but a parallel one which is livelier and more extravagant. They live—it is why we read them—not in the family and the shop, but in the world. They live to succeed extremely in the world. For even Fox and Bunyan succeed: they inherit the heavenly riches. And why should they not succeed? Remove the belief in success, material or spiritual, from Puritanism and you remove its mainspring and its political meaning. An unsuccessful Puritan is the disappointed sectary snapping sourly at his neighbours because he is unable to get the better of them.

Still, at first sight, the great Puritan autobiographers are an unlovely crowd. They have the vitality of weeds. We read them for their realism and their eccentricity. But would we choose their company now? Only two among those names might transplant into the twentieth century: Cobbett because he might fit in with the Napoleonic pattern of our time, and the other is Benjamin Franklin. Franklin is the only certain choice. One thinks of him as the first of the civilised Puritans. With his urbanity, his humour, his sagacity, his scientific adventurousness and his political vision, he can easily be transplanted, though he would loll like some dog's-eared and old-fashioned compendium of good sense and information in our businesslike world of isolated specialists. To entertain him would be like entertaining one of our founders.

The Franklin literature is a large one. Among recent *Lives*, Carl Van Doran's is the most thorough, sympathetic and readable. There is also an intelligent study by a Frenchman done in 1929: *Benjamin Franklin, Bourgeois d'Amérique*. But the reader should go first of all for the accent and flavour of the subject and begin with Franklin's own story. The World's Classics edition has the advantage of including a complete example from his famous *Almanac of Poor Richard*, which was enjoyed by thousands in America and which made D. H. Lawrence so angry. Lawrence's attack on Franklin in his *Studies in Classical American Literature* ought to be read, but it is a typical misfire. Lawrence, one supposes, could not forgive another Puritan for knowing more about sex than he did, and before Franklin's irony, urbanity and benevolence, Lawrence cuts an absurd figure, rather like that of a Sunday School teacher who has gone to a social dressed up as a howling dervish, when fancy dress was *not* requested. There is of course *something* in Lawrence's diatribe; it is the criticism by the man whose life is all poetry of the man whose life is all prose.

The reader of Franklin's autobiography must be struck by the way the Puritans hang together. Defoe and Bunyan were Franklin's first instructors. Defoe and Franklin have also similar origins; they were both the sons of tallow chandlers, and Defoe's *Essay on Projects* was one of the books which had a lasting influence on Franklin's mind. The resemblances between their careers are simply resemblances of class. The chief difference between the two shopkeepers appears when we observe the benevolence of the American's mind, the flow of imagination that transforms the pawky philosophy of go-getting and self-interest. Defoe was a retailer to the end; Franklin was a wholesaler. His plans, his experiments, his political actions are not part of his career; they flow beyond himself upon society. We feel that with all its toughness, resource and courage Defoe's character was a narrow one and incapable of growth, and there is, in fact, his dubious middle phase as a spy. Franklin, on the other hand, expands. His life reminds one, as the life of Cobbett does, how good the American climate was for the English character at this period; for if Franklin got ideas from Defoe, his style from Addison, his irony from Socrates and the stimulus to his genius from France of the eighteenth century, he owed the enlargement of his nature to America. Without that he might still have been thought one of the greatest *savants* of his time, but he would not have been thought the most able or the most likeable.

As a life story the *Autobiography* is interesting for its events. It is far more interesting as a remarkable piece of amusing and considered self-portraiture. The best autobiographies are those which draw the writer's character full-face, and Franklin adds to this the capacity to describe the growth of his character. In one sense (the sense that D. H. Lawrence hated) the book is another success story, an early instalment of Samuel Smiles. How he sat up late to study, how he became a vegetarian to save money for books, how he watched his chances at the printers, twigged a trick or two from the Socratic method of innocent enquiry, bargained over an offer of marriage and at last earned enough money to eat his porridge out of a china bowl with a silver spoon, after years of earthenware and a wooden one—such stuff is apt to be despised by those who find themselves deeply interested by it against their wills. And if Franklin had left his narrative like that he would have been just one more successful mayor. But his belief in self-improvement, though deep, has an ironic inflection:

> It would not be altogether absurd if a man were to thank God for his vanity among the other comforts of life.

Such intimate and persuasive asides give a leisured shade to the blatant walls of Self-Help where, too often, one is asked to admire the placing of each unweathered brick. But there is more than the irony of an experienced old man looking back on his life in this story. We are shown the making of a mind, the formation of a temperament. The two qualities of Franklin are the variety of his interests and the originality of his intellect. He is always performing feats. There are the feats of brain, like the decision to learn the French, Spanish and Italian languages in middle age in order to prepare himself to learn Latin—and a very good short cut to Latin that is, too. There are the feats of citizenship: he started the first fire brigade, the first police force, the first system of street lighting in the American colonies, the earliest philosophical society and the earliest public library. His edition of *Pamela* was the first novel to be published there also. And there are the feats of invention which are famous, such as his investigation of dyes and his invention of a heating stove; an invention which pops up impishly between the great affair of the lightning rod and his theories about the paths of storms and earthquakes. And, all the time, this is the man who once swam from Chelsea to Blackfriars, working out a new system of swimming as he went, and was only saved by chance from setting up for life as a swimming instructor. Franklin's inventive faculty was directed even to working out a system, rather like book-keeping, for improving his moral character. He invented even new prayers.

Being a romantic, Lawrence imagined that Franklin's devotion to Use, Method and Order indicated the dreary objectives of his genius. They were its starting points, its immense stimulus. Against egotism—Lawrence's "the self is a dark forest"—Franklin put the citizen and the *savant*, and the emotion generated by being a lively citizen in a new society released an exuberant creative capacity in Franklin which was certainly no less than the creative force which Lawrence and many others have thought to lie in sex alone. The jeers of

Lawrence might have struck home had they been directed at estimable and lesser Self-Helpers, for the Self-Helper is usually a copyist only who ends by being all help and no self. Franklin was never a copyist. Least of all was he a copyist in sex—Lawrence's own speciality. Here (far from being the prudent shopkeeper) Franklin entered upon a marriage which was only "a common law" marriage and which may have been bigamous, not out of self-interest, but because his moral sensibility demanded it. Franklin understood the dangers of repressing the moral sense. And then, lest one be deceived into thinking the considerate, the businesslike and the robust are incompatibles, there is his famous letter to a young man who is worried about women. Prudence directs (Franklin says) that if a young man must, for his health's sake, have a mistress, it is better that she shall be old, for she will be past childbearing—and besides, the older a woman the more grateful she is! One would need to be very cynical indeed to think that remarkable advice wholly cynical. One may hardly blame the age of Reason and Order for being reasonable and orderly, or the first of the modern planners for believing that all plans should be practical and should produce concrete benefits for society—stoves for the draughty New England rooms, fire brigades for wooden cities, political union for threatened states, prayers that will guide us "to our truest interest", and even discreet happiness for ladies past the prime of life.

THE AMERICAN PURITAN

AFTER reading Hemingway and Faulkner and speculating upon the breach of the American novel with its English tradition, we go back to the two decisive, indigenous Americans who opened the new vein—Mark Twain and Edgar Allan Poe. Everything really American, really non-English comes out of that pair of spiritual derelicts, those two scarecrow figures with their half-lynched minds. Both of them, but particularly Twain, represent the obverse side of Puritanism. We have never had this obverse in England, for the political power of Puritanism lasted for only a generation and has since always bowed if it has not succumbed to civilised orthodoxy. If an Englishman hated Puritanism, there was the rest of the elaborate English tradition to support him; but American Puritanism was totalitarian and if an American opposed it, he found himself alone in a wilderness with nothing but bottomless cynicism and humorous bitterness for his consolation. There has never been in English literature a cynicism to compare with the American; at any rate we have never had that, in some ways vital, but always sardonic or wretched, cynicism with its broken chopper edge and its ugly wound. We have also never had its by-product: the humorous philosophers; Franklin's Poor Richard, the Josh Billingses, the Artemus Wards, the Pudd'nhead Wilsons and Will Rogerses with their close-fisted proverbs:

"Training is everything. The peach was once a bitter almond: cauliflower is nothing but a cabbage with a college education."

Or:

"Consider well the proportion of things. It is better to be a young June bug than an old bird of Paradise."

I say we have never had this kind of thing, but there is one exception to prove the rule and to prove it very well, for he also is an uprooted and, so to speak, colonial writer. Kipling with his "A woman is always a woman, but a good cigar is a smoke" is our first American writer with a cynicism, a cigar-stained humour and a jungle book of beliefs which, I think, would be a characteristic of our literature if we become seriously totalitarian in the future. For English totalitarianism would create the boredom and bitterness of the. spiritual wilderness, as surely as Puritanism did in America.

When Mark Twain turned upon the religion of his child-hood because it was intolerable, he was unaware that it would destroy him by turning him into a money-grubber of the most disastrously Puritan kind. Fortunately the resources of the imagination are endless even when a fanatical philosophy wrecks human life, genius and happiness. Out of the mess which Twain made of his life, amid the awful pile of tripe which he wrote, there does rise one book which has the serenity of a thing of genius. *Huckleberry Finn* takes the breath away. Knowing his life, knowing the hell from which the book has ascended, one dreads as one turns from page to page the seem-ingly inevitable flop. How can so tortured and so angry a comedian refrain from blackguarding God, Man and Nature for the narrow boredom of his early life, and thus ruin the gurgling comedy and grinning horror of the story? But an imaginative writer appears to get one lucky break in his career; for a moment the conflicts are assimilated, the engine ceases to work against itself. The gears do not crash and *Huckleberry Finn* hums on without a jar. America gets its first and indis-putable masterpiece. The boyhood of Huck Finn is the boy-hood of a new culture and a new world.

The curious thing about *Huckleberry Finn* is, that although it is one of the funniest books in all literature and really astonishing in the variety of its farce and character, we are even more moved than we are amused by it.   Why are we moved?   Do we feel the sentiment of sympathy only?   Are we sighing with some envy and self-pity?   "Alas, Huck Finn is just what I would have been in my boyhood if I had had half a chance." Are we sorry for the vagrant, or are we moved by his rebellion? These minor feelings may play their part; but they are only sighs on the surface of the main stream of our emotion.   Twain has brought to his subject far more than this personal longing; he has become the channel of the generic American emotion which floods all really American literature—nostalgia.   In that brilliant, hit-or-miss book, *Studies in Classical American Literature*, which is either dead right or dead wrong, D. H. Lawrence called this feeling the longing of the rebel for a master.   It may be simply the longing for a spiritual home, but it is as strong in Mark Twain as it is implicit in Hemingway.   One finds this nostalgia in Anglo-Irish literature which is also colonial and, in a less lasting way, once again in the work of Kipling. The peculiar power of American nostalgia is that it is not only harking back to something lost in the past, but suggests also the tragedy of a lost future.   As Huck Finn and old Jim drift down the Mississippi from one horrifying little town to the next and hear the voices of men quietly swearing at one another across the water about "a chaw of tobacco"; as they pass the time of day with the scroungers, rogues, murderers, the lonely women, the frothing revivalists, the maundering boatmen and fantastic drunks, we see the human wastage that is left behind in the wake of a great effort of the human will, the hopes frustrated, the idealism which has been whittled down to eccentricity and mere animal cunning.   These people are the price paid for building a new country.   The human spectacle is there.   It is not, once you have faced it—which Dickens did not do in *Martin Chuzzlewit*, obsessed as he was by the negative pathos of the immigrant—it is not a disheartening spectacle; for the value of a native humour like Twain's is that it records a profound reality in human nature: the ability of man to adjust himself to any circumstance and somehow to survive and make a life.

Movement is one of the great consolers of human woe; movement, a process of continual migration is the history of America. It is this factor which gives Twain's wonderful descriptions of the journey down the Mississippi its haunting overtone and which, naturally enough, awakens a sensibility in him which is shown nowhere else in his writings and which is indeed vulgarly repressed in them:

> . . . then we set down on the sandy bottom where the water was about knee-deep and watched the daylight come. Not a sound anywhere—perfectly still—just like the whole world was asleep, only sometimes the bull-frogs a-clattering may be. The first thing to see, looking away over the water, was a kind of dull line—that was on the woods on t'other side—you couldn't make nothing else out; then a pale place in the sky; then more paleness, spreading around; then the river softened up, away off, and wasn't black any more but grey; you could see little dark spots drifting along, ever so far away—trading scows . . . and such things; and long black streaks—rafts; sometimes you could hear a sweep screaking; or jumbled-up voices, it was so still, and sounds come so far; and by-and-by you could see a streak on the water which you know by the look of the streak that there's a snag in the swift current which breaks on it and that streak looks that way; and you see the mist curl up off the water, and the east reddens up, and the river, and you make out a log cabin in the edge of the woods, away on the bank t'other side of the river, being a woodyard likely, and piled by them cheats so you can throw a dog through it anywheres. . . .

And afterwards we would watch the lonesomeness of the

river, and kind of lazy along and by-and-by, lazy off to sleep. Wake up, by-and-by, and look to see what done it, and may be see a steamboat, coughing along upstream, so far off towards the other side you couldn't tell nothing about her only whether she was sternwheel or side wheel; then for about an hour there wouldn't be nothing to hear nor nothing to see—just solid lonesomeness. Once there was a thick fog, and the rafts and things that went by was beating tin pans so the steam boats wouldn't run over them. A scow or a raft went by so close we could hear them talking and cussing and laughing—heard them plain; but we couldn't see no sign of them; it made you feel crawly, it was like spirits carrying on that way in the air. Jim said he believed it was spirits; but I says, "No, spirits wouldn't say 'dern this dem fog'."

(Note the word "way" in this passage; it is a key nostalgic word in the American vocabulary, vaguely vernacular and burdened with the associations of the half-articulate. It is a favourite Hemingway word, of course: "I feel *that way*"— not the how or what he feels of the educated man.)

The theme of *Huckleberry Finn* is the rebellion against civilisation and especially against its traditions:

I reckon I got to light out for the Territory ahead of the rest, because Aunt Sally she's going to adopt me and sivilize me and I can't stand it. I been there before.

Huck isn't interested in "Moses and the Bulrushers" because Huck "don't take no stock of dead people". He garbles European history when he is discussing Kings with Jim, the negro. Whether Huck is the kind of boy who will grow up to build a new civilisation is doubtful; Tom Sawyer obviously will because he is imaginative. Huck never imagines anything except fears. Huck is "low down plain ornery", always in trouble because of the way he was brought up with "Pap". He is a natural anarchist and bum. He can live without civilisation, depending on shrewd affections and loyalty to friends. He is the first of those typical American portraits of the underdog, which have culminated in the poor white literature and in Charlie Chaplin—an underdog who gets along on horse sense, so to speak. Romanticism, ideas, ideals are repugnant to Huck; he "reckons" he "guesses", but he doesn't think. In this he is the opposite of his hero, Tom Sawyer. Tom had been telling "stretchers" about arabs, elephants and Aladdin's lamp. Huck goes at once "into a brood".

> I thought all this over for two or three days, and then I reckoned I would see if there was anything in it. I got an old tin lamp and an irony ring and went out into the woods and rubbed it till I sweat like an Injun, calculating to build a palace and sell it; but it wasn't no use, none of the genies came. So then I judged that all that stuff was only just one of Tom Sawyer's lies. I reckoned he believed in the A-rabs and elephants, but as for me I think different. It has all the marks of a Sunday school.

That is, of American Puritan civilisation, the only civilisation he knew.

"Ornery", broody, superstitious, with a taste for horrors, ingenious, courageous without knowing it, natural, sound-hearted, philosophical in a homely way—those are the attributes of the gorgeous, garrulous Huck and they give a cruelly extravagant narrative its humanity. He obliges you to accept the boy as the devastating norm. Without him the violence of the book would be stark reporting of low life. For if *Huckleberry Finn* is a great comic book it is also a book of terror and brutality. Think of the scenes: Pap with d.t.'s chasing Huck round the cabin with a knife; Huck sitting up all night with a gun preparing to shoot the old man; Huck's early familiarity with corpses; the pig-killing scene; the sight of the frame house (evidently some sort of brothel) floating down the Mississippi with a murdered man in it; the fantastic events at the Southern house where two families shoot each other down in a vendetta; the drunken Boggs who comes into town to pick a quarrel and is eventually coolly shot dead before the eyes of his screaming young daughter by the man he has insulted. The "Duke" and "the King", those cynical rascals whose adventures liven up the second half of the story are sharpers, twisters and crooks of the lowest kind. Yet a child is relating all this with a child's detachment and with a touch of morbidity. Marvellous as the tale is, as a collection of picaresque episodes and as a description of the mess of frontier life, it is strong meat. Sometimes we wonder how Twain's public stomached such illusionless reporting. The farce and the important fact that in this one book Mark Twain never forced a point nor overwrote—in the Dickens way for example —are of course the transfiguring and beguiling qualities. His corpse and coffin humour is a dry wine which raises the animal spirits. Old Jim not only looked like a dead man after the "King" had painted him blue, but like one "who had been dead a considerable time".

Judiciousness is carried to the comic limit. And then, Mark Twain is always getting the atmosphere, whether he picks up the exact words of loafers trying to borrow tobacco off one another or tells a tall story of an hysterical revival meeting.

Atmosphere is the decisive word. *Huckleberry Finn* reeks of its world. From a sensitive passage like:

> When I got there it was all still and Sunday-like, and hot and the hands was gone to the fields; and there was them kind faint dronings of bugs and flies that makes it seem so lonesome and like everybody's dead. . . .

to descriptions of the silly, dying girl's ridiculous poetry, the sensibility draws a clear outline and is never blurred and turned into sentimentality. One is enormously moved by Huck's

181

view of the world he sees. It is the world not of Eden, but of the "old Adam", not the golden age of the past, but the earthly world of a reality which (we feel with regret) we have let slip through our fingers too carelessly. Huck is only a crude boy, but luckily he was drawn by a man whose own mind was arrested, with disastrous results in his other books, at the schoolboy stage; here it is perfect. And a thousand times better than the self-conscious adventures of Stevenson's *Treasure Island* and *Kidnapped*.

Is *Huckleberry Finn* one of the great works of picaresque literature? It is, granting the limits of a boy's mind in the hero and the author, a comic masterpiece; but this limitation is important. It is not a book which grows spiritually, if we compare it to *Quixote*, *Dead Souls* or even *Pickwick*; and it is lacking in that civilised quality which you are bound to lose when you throw over civilisation—the quality of pity. One is left with the cruelty of American humour, a cruelty which is softened by the shrewd moralisings of the humorous philosophers—the Josh Billingses, the Artemus Wards, the Will Rogerses. And once Mark Twain passed this exquisite moment of his maturity, he went to bits in that morass of sentimentality, cynicism, melodrama and vulgarity which have damned him for the adult reader.

THE QUAKER COQUETTE

I F there is not a novel in every man and woman we meet, there is at any rate a cautionary tale. "That ridiculous and excellent person, Mrs. Opie," said Miss Mitford. "What a miserable hash she has made of her existence." Somewhere in the world—so we may console ourselves when we feel ignored and forgotten—there is bound to be a Miss Mitford holding us up as an awful warning, using us as a frightful example of what can happen to a human being when he or she strays from the Mitford path. We have, of course, our bad moments and it must be agreed that Miss Mitford had caught the widow of Opie, the painter, at that point in middle age where so many women are clumsy with their cues and seem not to know in what play they are acting. After a life of triumphant gaiety in London and Paris, after writing a number of gaudy, guilty and improper books, the tantalising and beautiful widow had suddenly rejoined the Quaker circle in Norwich where she had passed her youth. She had put on the Quaker gown and bonnet, she had started writing very boring, didactic tales and went about thee-ing and thou-ing her embarrassed acquaintances with all the gush of a convert and all the bounce of a reformed sinner. Norwich raised its eyebrows. The good may cry Hallelujah when the lost soul repents and returns to the fold, but there is often a touch of disappointment not to mention suspicion in the cry, for where would the good be if there were no sinners left to hearten them on their hard pilgrimage? At Earlham, the home of Elizabeth Fry and the Gurney family who thought they knew their Amelia so well, such doubts could not be concealed. A

Quaker—but wasn't Mrs. Opie still a friend of Lady Cork's? Hadn't she still got in her drawer the manuscript of an unfortunate novel? Could one credit the champion of Mary Wollstonecraft and Godwin with a change of heart? What prospect was there of "the inner light" shining for long in a mind bedizened with the memories of fashionable society, of "pink" parties for the gay and "blue" parties for the highbrow? Wasn't Amelia Opie congenitally "shallow"? Her conversation might even be a leg pull, for she did seem to have what George Fox would have called (in the century before Quakerism became mellow), a "light and chaffy" nature. But neither the Quakers nor Miss Mitford could take the severe view of Mrs. Opie's vivacious character for long. They loved her too well to regard her finally as the awful warning against worldliness. And the truth is that Amelia Opie had not so much the awfulness of a warning as the piquancy of a recurrent type. Born in 1769 and dying in 1853 she had fed on ideologies. She had lived through a revolution and a European war, and then had repented. Today her kind of character and repentance has become common if not yet modish. Mrs. Opie is a kind of heroine of our time.

What is the type? Amelia was a flirt, a highbrow flirt. She was the adored and adoring daughter of a Norwich doctor. Her mother had been an invalid for years and when she died the girl was still in her teens. She became her father's hostess. When one goes into the question of her coquetry one comes immediately upon that so common decision of Nature that girls who have an inordinate devotion to their fathers shall deal coolly and indecisively with other men or shall prefer those who are much younger or much older than themselves. Add to this the intellectual tastes of Amelia's father and one finds a young lady who coquettes with literature, politics and religion and calls them in to aid her in the more important business of catching men. Her susceptible nature—it was susceptible rather than passionate—made her into one of those women who, when they come into a room, shine with the certainty that they will succeed and the lightness of their feeling makes them do so. Later she was to harden into the vivacious snob and to fatten into the determined celebrity hunter who bosomed her way into the limelight with the infallible flair of the woman who knew her geniuses.

Being irresistible was not only an instinct but a business with Amelia Opie. She wrote frightful novels which made Sir Walter Scott weep, and awful verses which Sydney Smith quoted in his lectures—the bad taste of great men has a long history—but she had taken care, it might be observed, to get to know the great first. She asked Southey once to say a word to the reviewers. She was one of those women who, having addled a man's judgment by making herself physically desirable, like an ice on a hot day, then change about and insist on being admired for their minds. She was quite candid about this technique in her last novel. She was irresistible, she says, because she was herself unable to resist—at first; she began resisting only when, by flattering them, she had made others think they had become irresistible themselves. No grand passions for her, she said, no durable affections. "My object is to amuse life away and *a little love*, just enough to give interest to scenes and places, is delightful. . . . My attachments are like gentle squeezes of the hand." A great passion would destroy her "peace of mind". No wonder the Norwich Quakers, plump, benevolent but trimly literal in matters of virtue, were a little dubious when the chatty best seller who knew all the celebrities of London and Paris, put on the Quaker bonnet. Was the accomplished actress just putting on another act? Of course she was. And yet, of course, she was not. Amelia had some of that stupidity in her nature which some call ingenuousness. It is the price a woman has to pay for being vain of her unconventionality. But Amelia is a delightful argument for the charm of an ill-adjusted life, for the attraction of being a bit of a fraud and for a dash of the prude in the wanton female character.

During the many years of her mother's illness, Amelia's childhood had been one of solitude and constraint. She was shut away, silenced, ignored. Imagination awakened. She quickly picked up a love of the sensational, the guilty and the morbid. The effect of the death of her mother was to release Amelia suddenly from a world of dark, dramatic and lugubrious brooding into a world of sociability and light. The late eighteenth century was made for escapades of the mind, and many of the English provincial towns had the intellectual liveliness of little capitals. In Norwich, Crome was painting. Holcroft, Godwin and the Radical leaders dined with the doctor. The ideas of the French Revolution were in the air and, as she listened to her father's praise of Lafayette, the young hostess became a republican at a bound. Alone in her room, she began to write plays and poetry and when she had done a few pages she found that great men liked to be asked for their criticisms. At least, with young ingenuity, she *thought* that this was what interested them. Her mind (she was to tell Godwin and Holcroft as they looked with desire upon her person) was her chief preoccupation. It is a weakness of intellectuals to be interested in minds and Amelia's fervid talk about hers was the ideal bait; ideal because it hooked the listener and yet kept him threshing away unavailingly at a safe distance, at the end of the line. With Godwin hooked, with Godwin jealous of her friends, begging her to rule her emotions by the light of Reason while he himself fell into an irrational condition because she would not kiss him, Amelia's technique was established. Now she could deal with anyone, indeed preferably with several at a time. She sat down to write an anonymous book called *The Dangers of Coquetry*.

In the meantime she had made another conquest, one which

lasted her lifetime and which did not spring from her engaging vanity but was directed by a warmer need of her nature. As a child Amelia had not known the geniality of normal family life. She needed a family and she conquered one. The Gurneys of Earlham were Quakers, a large family of children younger than herself and glad to admire and love the literary belle with her poems and her song. Quakerism had softened; music, painting and dancing were permitted to the younger Gurneys who turned to Amelia with all the love which the prim feel for the worldly. The young Gurneys were in revolt against their traditions, its politics, its culture. Where was there not revolt in that generation? There were Corresponding Societies—the English equivalent of the Jacobin Clubs—in Norwich, respectable "pinks" were being spied on and even tried for sedition, treason and revolutionary activity; even the religious faith of the younger Gurneys was lapsing. To Amelia who was "in the movement" and who had run into scandal because of her passion for Mary Wollstonecraft and her defence of Godwin's marriage, they turned as to a goddess. The fact that she was known by now to be in love with a married man brought even brighter confidence to the agony of the young atheists. They were to get their own back later when time brought their repentance, and Amelia, the converter was to be reconverted by them. Elizabeth Fry was one of those children and Amelia, at her gayest and most "worldly", in the midst of writing her "immoral" novels about seduced heroines, mad fathers and women ruined by "a false step", always responded uncomfortably to criticism from Earlham.

But this quaint fruit of Amelia's deep affection for the Gurneys was to ripen slowly. By the time she was 28 and still unmarried Norwich had begun to shake its head. It was all very well to be clever, beautiful, mysterious, the skilful heartbreaker (Norwich said), but the coquette who turns down one proposal too many ends on the shelf. And Amelia was in her first mess. "Mr. B.", the married man, was only too well married and there was no way of getting him. It was a crisis of the heart; it was, even more, a crisis for her vanity with all Norwich watching, the Gurneys above all. The solution was—and how true to her type she was—to drown a scandal in a sensation. She did so. The elegant young provincial married Opie. Opie was a peasant with a strong Cornish accent, shocking table manners, a divorced wife. Amelia did not love him. But he was a fashionable painter and thoroughly in the limelight. His table manners made her hesitate—odd things made her hesitate in her life: after Opie's death she went all out for a peer with the idea of reforming him and turned him down in the end because "they both had enough to live on"—but in the end she plunged. She married Opie. She pushed him into society, saw to it that he got commissions. Now it was that she wrote. When her husband's work went temporarily out of fashion she buckled to and wrote a best-seller. And when he died—for the marriage was a short interlude in her life—she fought to get him buried in St. Paul's Cathedral and grieved so extravagantly, in so many poems, panegyrics, memoirs, and so loudly that her friends had to remind her that she was enjoying herself more than the onlookers.

The Gurneys were worried. They enjoyed being stirred up by the celebrity, though by this time Amelia's claim to have a mind was mocked by reviewers. The Gurneys were older. They had returned to respectable opinions and even to their old religion. A reconquest of the Gurneys was necessary, a new disturbing of their godliness. To this period belongs her characteristic affair with Joseph John Gurney, a strict young Quaker, and with Haydon, the elderly reprobate of Bognor, who had had a notorious *ménage à trois* with his wife and his servant. To Joseph John she talked and wrote about "the world", a subject which shocked and fascinated

188

him; to Haydon, she talked about religion, which shocked and fascinated *him*. Haydon was old, Joseph John was young. He listened, he reproved, he lectured. Amelia loved it. She was delighted that he did not despair of bringing her back into the fold. It would have dismayed her to know that the prudent Quaker would succeed in recapturing her for the Lord, but would be careful to marry someone else.

The second mess, "the miserable hash" in fact, was the direct cause of her conversion. Sooner or later that amusing vanity, that too clever susceptibility, was certain to be snubbed. One does not suppose she loved Tom Alderson, her knowing young cousin, very deeply, but she was humiliated when he turned her down. The answer again was a new sensation: the Quaker bonnet. We need not agitate ourselves, as the Quakers did, about the sincerity of that conversion. At 60 when she broke out again and went to Paris on a celebrity hunt after Lafayette and to renew her revolutionary enthusiasms, D'Angers the sculptor called her a Janus, a two-faced syren who instinctively showed you the profile you did not ask for. Her misleading Puritanism, so perfectly chaste but with delusive promise of wantonness, delighted the Frenchman. But Miss Mitford cattily noted that Amelia ordered the silk for her Quaker gown from Paris; and Paris was astonished and enchanted by a celebrity who arrived in the disguise of the Meeting House. It was all in character. In her youth she had stood in court watching the trial of Holcroft for treason and had cried, Liberty in the streets; but she had insisted on meeting the aristocratic *émigrés* too.

And how misleading she is even in her portraits. The plump, soft, wistful wench with the murmuring eyes and sensual mouth, in Opie's painting, does not look like the dazzler of the great. The humorous, blunt-faced, double-chinned sexagenarian of D'Anger's medallion does not look like the spiritualised creature which his ecstatic letters describe.

What was it that got them all? Was it the famous technique, the flattery of the perpetual promise? Or the most flattering of all flatteries, the most active and subtle of the social arts (as indeed the last of her "unredeemed" novels suggested), the art of listening? For one cannot, one must not, believe that the title of the first book, written after her redemption, offers the clue. It was a didactic work entitled *Lying, In all its Branches*.

LIST OF WORKS REFERRED TO IN TEXT

ADOLPHE. Benjamin Constant. Edited by Gustave Rudler. *Manchester University Press.*

LE CAHIER ROUGE. Benjamin Constant. *Calmann-Levy.*

TURGENEV. THE MAN AND HIS ART. Avrahm Yarmolinsky. *Hodder & Stoughton.*

RUDIN. Ivan Turgenev; translated by Constance Garnett. *Wm. Heinemann.*

THE EARLY VICTORIAN NOVELISTS. Lord David Cecil. *Constable.*

WIVES AND DAUGHTERS. Mrs. Gaskell. *Everyman & World's Classics.*

NORTH AND SOUTH. Mrs. Gaskell. *Everyman & World's Classics.*

MARY BARTON. Mrs. Gaskell. *Everyman & World's Classics.*

THE POSSESSED. Fyodor Dostoevski; translated by Constance Garnett. *Heinemann.*

DOSTOEVSKI. Ernest J. Simmons. *Oxford University Press.*

DOSTOEVSKY. E. H. Carr. *Allen & Unwin.*

DEAD SOULS. By Nickolai Gogol; translated by D. J. Hogarth. *Everyman.*

MÉMOIRES OF EUGÈNE-FRANÇOIS VIDOCQ. 2 vols. *Librairie Grund.*

MÉMOIRES OF EUGÈNE-FRANÇOIS VIDOCQ. 4 vols. 1829.

LIFE OF VIDOCQ. Jagot. *Stock.*

JUDE THE OBSCURE. Thomas Hardy. *Macmillan.*

UNDER THE GREENWOOD TREE. Thomas Hardy. *Macmillan.*

GERMINAL. Émile Zola; translated by Havelock Ellis. *Everyman.*

ZOLA. Henri Barbusse. *Dent.*

GIL BLAS DE SANTILLANE. Le Sage. *Garnier.*

THE AUTOBIOGRAPHIES OF EDWARD GIBBON. Introduced by Lord Sheffield. Edited by John Murray.

AUTOBIOGRAPHY. Edward Gibbon. Notes by Lord Sheffield. *Everyman.*

EDWARD GIBBON. D. M. Low. *Chatto & Windus.*

JONATHAN WILD. Henry Fielding. *Everyman & World's Classics.*

KILVERT'S DIARY. Edited by William Plomer. 3 vols. *Cape.*

JOURNAL. George Fox. *Everyman.*

ENGLAND UNDER THE STUARTS. G. M. Trevelyan. *Methuen.*

PLAYS AND PROSE. J. M. Synge. *Everyman.*

SYNGE. P. P. Howe. *Martin Secker.*

A HERO OF OUR OWN TIME. M. Y. Lermontov; translated by Eden and Cedar Paul. *Allen & Unwin.*

THE RING AND THE BOOK. Robert Browning. *Oxford University Press.*

GULLIVER'S TRAVELS. Jonathan Swift. *Everyman.*

DIARY OF A NOBODY. George and Weedon Grossmith. *Everyman.*

HISTORY OF A CONSCRIPT OF 1813: WATERLOO. Erckmann-Chatrian; translated by Russell D. Gillmann. *Everyman.*

THE STORY OF A PEASANT. Erckmann-Chatrian. 2 vols. C. J. Hogarth. *Everyman.*

AMELIA, THE TALE OF A PLAIN FRIEND. Jacobine Menzies-Wilson and Helen Lloyd. *Oxford University Press.*

THREE NOVELS. Thomas Love Peacock. *Nelson.*

THE CONFESSIONS OF ZENO. Italo Svevo; translated by Beryl de Zoete. *Putnam.*

AS A MAN GROWS OLDER. Italo Svevo; translated by Beryl de Zoete. *Putnam.*

THE NICE OLD MAN AND THE PRETTY GIRL. Italo Svevo; translated by L. Collison Morley. *Hogarth.*

VANITY FAIR. W. M. Thackeray. *Everyman.*

HUCKLEBERRY FINN. Mark Twain. *Chatto & Windus.*

PUDD'NHEAD WILSON. Mark Twain. *Chatto & Windus.*

MARK TWAIN. Edgar Lee Masters. *Scribner's.*

AUTOBIOGRAPHY OF BENJAMIN FRANKLIN. *World's Classics.*

BENJAMIN FRANKLIN. Carl Van Doran. *Putnam.*

BENJAMIN FRANKLIN: BOURGEOIS D'AMÉRIQUE.